STONEGATE

A PLACE WITHOUT TIME

Eliana, Hope you enjoy the book. Thank you. It's so nice knowing you!

Paul A Merkel

PAUL MERKEL

Hope you enjoy the book. It's so nice to know you! Thank you.

ISBN 978-1-64079-890-8 (paperback)
ISBN 978-1-64079-891-5 (digital)

Christian Faith Publishing, Inc.
832 Park Avenue
Meadville, PA 16335
www.christianfaithpublishing.com

Printed in the United States of America

DEDICATION

This book is dedicated to the three greatest miracles of my life, my daughters Madison and Mariah along with their mother Amanda.

It was a most wonderful season.

To think that God loves you even more than I do, takes my breath away and renders me completely speechless.

ACKNOWLEDGEMENT

To John D Merkel

Dad, without you this book would still be only a thought in the far regions of my mind. You helped call it forward and into existence. You believed in me and it's birth long before I was able. Thank you for your guidance, support, wisdom, and painstaking skill, as you walked me through this journey from start to finish. I am so very proud to call you Dad.

FOREWORD

One night of choices leads to a lifetime of consequences... This is based on the real-life story of my friend Paul's journey through high security prison as a result of a vehicle collision while impaired by alcohol. The reader accompanies Paul on his journey of transformation and ultimately becomes a partner in his mission to prevent all young people from driving a car while impaired or riding with someone who is. While a police officer in a local high school in Alaska, I partnered with Paul to get this message to our youth by sharing the real-life consequences of drinking and driving through a prevention program called *"Every 15 Minutes."* This riveting personal account has an important message that I hope will positively impact the decisions made by the next generation of drivers.

Wendi Shackelford
Police officer (retired)
Anchorage (AK) Police Department

ONE

It's around 2:00 a.m., and I still can't fall sleep. It's my first night in the Arizona State Penitentiary. I arrived late this afternoon. So much has happened today that it's really hard to wind down from it all. I'm a little scared at the moment, anticipating what's to come.

I have two windows in my cell that look out to the back side of the prison. They are small, only about four feet high and four inches wide. Only one eye can see out at a time, so depth perception is kind of hard. Outside my windows, you can see the fences and lots of razor wire. Rows of it. The whole area is lit up by huge lights on top of extremely tall poles. They're shining so bright that it's almost like daytime out there.

I'm up about fifteen feet from the sandy ground below. The sand is raked in straight semisecret lines all the way to the first fence. That's so footprints will show up if someone was to get out there, which would be impossible.

Every pair of shoes an inmate has must have a *V* notched out on the inside step of the sole. That way, DOC can track you if need be. When you walk in the dirt, you can see the notch on the footprint. Immediately it's known as an inmate's shoeprint.

I can see the first fence pretty good as I sit here looking out. The razor wire starts at the ground and goes up the fence about ten feet. It also sticks out about four feet from the fence. It would be extremely hard to reach the first fence, let alone climb it. At the top of this first fence, which is thirty feet high, is even more razor wire,

11

big shiny hoops of it. It also hangs down from the top of the fence about ten feet.

Then there is what's called no-man's-land. This is the ground sandwiched between the first and the second fence. No-man's-land is about fifty feet wide. It also has raked lines in the sand to see footprints. There are also electric eyes, trip wires, cameras, and who knows what else they might have out there.

The second fence has the same amount of razor wire as the first fence. There's also an armed guard driving a pickup truck around the perimeter of the prison. The two fences and no-mans-land circle around the whole prison. It's kind of like a moat going around a castle. To top it all off, there are gun towers on the corners of the prison yard.

This prison yard is one of three other yards that sit on this prison property. My yard/prison is really just a prison inside a prison. The prison yard is outside my cell door. When my door opens, I'm basically in the yard but still up on the second tier. There are only two tier levels here. My cell number is B22.

Right now I can see car lights moving along the highway. It's only about a half-mile away from this tease of a window I have. The cars are going east and west, and it seems all night, they pass one after another. Clueless that a convict is envying them, whoever they are. All I can think about is, "Do they know how good they've got it out there?"

I'm thinking some of them are heading for California and will most likely be on the beach by noon today. God would I give my right arm for that right now. Why in the world didn't I take advantage of the life and chances I had when I was a free man? Instead, I'm sitting in this dirt hole of a prison with a bunch of wannabe gangsters who couldn't care less if they even get out.

Why in the world am I here? What went so wrong? When and where did I make such a bad turn in life to wind up here? I guess I really didn't look to see where I was going. Like they say, "All roads lead to somewhere."

I know now I had it *all* out there. The good life. I had a pretty good upbringing on the north shore suburbs just outside of Chicago.

I went to some of the best schools in the country there. I had a family that loved and cared for me, and I always had more then what I needed growing up. I had a great job, a few good friends, a little money in the bank, and a really nice place to live. I could even travel whenever I wanted to. I had the things that most people just dream about. And still here I am. It's amazing how fast it all washed down the drain.

It's as if I woke up from the American dream and found myself in this nightmare of reality. God, I never thought that at age twenty-five I'd be in this place. I sure took the life I had for granted.

What really hurts is some of those cars I'm watching are on their way to Phoenix. That's where my brokenhearted girlfriend and other good friends are living. And at this very minute, they are in their safe, cozy, comfortable beds, fast asleep, dreaming sweet dreams and resting well.

God I wish I'd just wake up from this whole thing, and it would be just a bad, bad dream. Like in that movie with Scrooge. I'd wake up and say, "Merry Christmas to all!" I'd be smiling from ear to ear, happy to be alive. And now knowing the truth of what really matters in life. Full of gratitude and joy, ready to live life to its fullest.

But this is not going to happen. This is my life now. I know this is where I belong. I'll say that again, so there'll be no misunderstanding.

I belong in prison.

My cell mate, David, who's on the bottom bunk, is fast asleep. And though there's someone in here with me, I still can't help but feel totally alone. Alone like never before. Like I'm the only person on earth and everyone else has left for heaven. But I alone was forgotten. God, are you still there? Have you forgotten me? Are you so mad at me that you've let me go? I know it was a horrible thing that happened and that I need to be in this place of pain and separation. But please don't turn from me. Please help me to make things right with you. Somehow. Some day.

I can't help those guys that were hurt. And nothing will change it from already happening. I know they're in pain and that their lives have changed forever. God help them to fully recover and take care of them. Help them also to not hate me, not for too long at least.

Yes, I have become the bad guy. Nothing's going to change that; that's just the way it is. I do hope, though, that they fully recover and that nothing changes that.

As I sit here on the top bunk staring out my window into the free world, I can't help but think how bad I messed up my life. It was going so well, and now it's changed forever. My poor family and friends, God did I ever let them down. I really feel like crying tonight, but that won't happen, that's for sure. And most likely won't for a long, long time.

The first night in prison is a tough one. My mind is having trouble grabbing the reality that this place is now my home.

My cell is only about eight feet by ten feet, and it feels almost like a cave when you're in here. It's closed-in and dark, and even a little mysterious. The place has history, but it's not going to tell you of it. And it holds a feeling of real suspense. You feel the depth of uncertainty as you sit inside here.

It's as if I'm walking in a dark cave with only a flashlight, not knowing what's around the next corner. If you've ever been in a cave, you'd know it has that closed-in feeling to it. You always keep looking back to make sure you don't get too far from the entrance. So you can find your way out again. Well, in here, you keep looking at your cell door like it's getting farther away. And you're going to get lost if you don't keep your eye on it. You know it's the only way out, but you still do it anyway. I know it's small in here, but it feels like you just don't want to get too far from the way you came in. It's crazy what games your mind will play on you, once you're in here.

It also feels very solid and strong in here, like you could hit the wall with a sledgehammer, and it would only make a very low thud sound. The walls must be at least two feet thick and are definitely indestructible.

It's really not big enough for two people to be living in, especially in a place like this. The sink and toilet are right next to each other in the corner by the door. If you're on the toilet (which has no toilet seat, it's all steel) and someone opened the door (your cell-mate), you'd get the door in your face. Or if you would like to brush your teeth as your cellmate is on the toilet, you'll be standing next to him with all its liabilities.

To the left of the sink is the bottom bunk, which runs the length of the cell. The top bunk runs the width of the cell, at the backend of the cell. And under the top bunk, opposite the bottom bunk, there's a steel desk. All are bolted into the wall.

The mattress is a wonderful thing. If you're a cow or a horse or some other kind of barn animal, you'd be loving it. It's only about two inches thick, and it feels like it's filled with sand or some other kind of nonflammable material. The only other thing that I've ever slept on that's harder than this is concrete.

The block walls are cool and smooth to the touch. They haven't been painted in who knows how long, but right now, they're a dark and dirty mustard yellow color. Really depressing.

But what hits me the most is this out-of-place, but not so out-of-place, larger-than-life, very colorful life-like picture. It's on the whole wall over David's bed. It's this very beautiful and inviting naked woman. I'm not sure if it's a good thing to have a cell mate who's an artist with colored pencils. But it sure beats the other three dirty walls.

I really need to sleep. But I can't stop going over what's happened the last few months. Then it all hits me. Something that's so profound, it's hard for my brain to grab. I will be in prison for years! And life, as I've known it, is gone—totally gone. It will never ever be the same again.

As I'm lying here half asleep, my mind keeps drifting off to some of the last few moments I had in the free world. It was only a month ago, but it feels like a lifetime ago. The day was June 12. Another beautiful day in Arizona. My best buddy Craig and I were driving down the road, laughing about some of the good old days, like this one time in Mexico.

Craig was building a house down there, and from time to time, I'd go down there to help out. We had finished our work for the day and had eaten our camp stove dinner of hotdogs and beans. We were kicking back, drinking some Nescafé coffee and talking.

Only half of the roof was on the house at this point. It was like camping outside but with four-block walls around us and a door. The sky was always full of stars down there. It was still kind of early, but neither one of us felt much like playing cards by the lantern light that night.

Earlier that day, our friend Richard was being kind of a jerk and left to go back to his newly bought house just across the street. He was also helping out on Craig's house but would always seem to get lost when the work got hard.

After finishing my coffee, I said, "Hey, Craig, let's go try out those new bottle rockets we bought yesterday." Craig just smiled as we both scrambled for the door like a couple of ten-year-old boys.

The first rocket went quickly into the night sky and seemed to hang there for a moment before finally bursting into a colorful fireball, lighting up the pitch-black sky. After about twenty minutes and a few dozen bottle rockets, we were just about ready to turn in for the night.

We both kind of chuckled as I picked up the Coke bottle and laid it on the mound of sand that was holding it up, so that now it was pointing directly at Richard's house.

Craig's face went quickly from laughing and smiling to "Oh my god, no!" I'm not sure what I was thinking, but it was too late now. I had lit the fuse and a fast one at that. The rocket went off with what seemed to be a vengeance of its own, and the timing of the blast was almost perfect. It blew up about five feet over Richard's house and covered the palm leaf roof with fiery sparks. We couldn't believe it didn't immediately catch the house on fire and burn the whole place down. But thank God it didn't.

But what did happen though was still pretty bad. Richard's horses, which were tied up out front of his house, got so scared from the blast just over their heads that they ran off with such force, they pulled out their tie-down post and half of the front porch with it! .

Craig and I ran off like a couple of scared kids as if no one was going to know it was us. We were both laughing so hard that we practically crawled back into the door of the house. Craig was a little scared and peeked outside a few times before settling into his bag for the night. He wanted to make sure Richard's house was still okay and not on fire. I just lay in my sleeping bag and laughed myself to sleep.

I woke up the next morning to see Richard walking way out in the middle of the desert. You could barely see him out there, but you could hear him yelling and cursing, mad as he could be, trying to catch those horses. He'd get pretty close to them, and they'd run off even farther.

Craig and I were working on the roof that morning, watching Richard and laughing about the whole thing. He was out there for almost two hours, going crazy chasing those horses. Finally, the horses got tired of playing their game, and the two of them walked right past Richard, just out of his reach, and back to his house. Man, we thought that was funny. Richard knew he had it coming to him, so we didn't feel too bad about it all. Believe it or not, we were all pretty good friends. And for some reason or another, when we were together, we always brought the little kid out in each other. So anyway, here Craig and I we are driving down the road, laughing and telling old stories like this, when all of a sudden Craig gets this real serious look on his face and says, "You sure you want to keep going?"

I knew what he meant. And I always did like Mexico, but I needed to get this thing over with, one way or another. Six months of waiting to know my punishment was making me crazy. I didn't ask him, but I think Craig was just kidding and checking to see if I was ready to face my life and what I had done, and whatever was to come from it. You see, this was no ordinary day. It was my sentencing day. It had taken months since my last court date. I knew I could run for Mexico, but what kind of life would that be? The presentencing/probation report said that I had a good chance of getting house arrest, or maybe even community service work.

So I said, "I think we'd better just keep heading for the courthouse," though in the back of my mind I was still contemplating the worst that could happen that day. This time, I could possibly be leaving the courthouse wearing chains.

It's really quite terrifying to think about your life of freedom ending with just a tap of the judge's hammer. It's a lot like this: You woke up this morning, had your coffee, did all your morning stuff,

17

and then left your home. You don't know this leaving, but it's the last time you're going to be there. All those other things—like that pile of wash that needs to be done, your mail in the box, your bills on the desk, your trash in the kitchen, your money in the bank, and your book on the bedside table—will have to wait for (hopefully) someone else to take care of for you. Because you're not going to be there.

Sometime during your "today," you get taken away and put into a jail cell. The life you've lived up until this moment is now gone. They won't let you get back to your life to take care of these things, and they don't seem understand how desperately you need to.

No matter how hard you try or cry, you can't find your way back. It's now all just a dream. You can't seem to grasp the thought that you're still alive, but your (old) life is over. And as that thought is trying to find a place in your head to rest, you're hit with the soul-piercing reality that out there on the other side of this prison realm, life, as you've known it, is still moving, still living, and still loving.

When this thought completely surrounds you, you now know the pure and true agony of the prison life.

This is when slow panic sets in. Like having a small hole in the boat, it's just a matter of time, and you know you're going under.

Instinctively you understand that the longer you're away, the more difficult it will be to belong there once again. It's as if you and your loved ones were stranded on a desert island. The rescue boat comes, but it only has room for them. You're left on the shore waving good-bye as they get farther and farther out to sea. Slowly they fade through the distant horizon, and you can't see them anymore. They're gone. You sit down in the sand and start crying, altogether knowing that time passing can never be returned.

TWO

The most jail time I ever did was a few days, and mostly as a kid. Though I did that a few times, it was nothing like what I was facing now.

As we walked into the court house that day, I saw my refection in the glass door. I was trying to look the best I could. I had on my good black slacks with a nice crisp clean button down white shirt, and a new tie. But I was already sweating and not looking that good at all. I was really starting to get scared. As we walked down the long echoing hallway to the elevators, I quietly handed Craig my gold cross ring and asked him to hold it for me, just in case. Craig is like a brother to me. He's also like a father to me. I don't know how else to say it.

Looking back, I think my spirit knew I was not going home that day. But my mind would have nothing to do with the thought.

When I walked into the courtroom, I really had no idea what was about to happen. And not just with the court case, but within my own mind. As I walked up to the judge's bench, I felt like I was heading to the guillotines ready to lose my head. It was very surreal.

The judge started reading out loud, case numbers and all kinds of other things to do with my case. I really wasn't listening well because it all seemed to be just a blur of words with no real meaning to it.

Suddenly my mind jumped to attention. I heard the judge say, with each word spoken as if he had a mouth packed full of molasses,

"I sentence you to confinement in the Arizona State Department of Corrections for the term of…four years."

My mind about snapped. Trying to process it was like trying to read a blank page in a book. There was nothing there, nothing at all. The only thing I knew for sure was that my life just changed. When I could grab reality again, I heard myself crying and felt my body shaking. I was terrified. When I looked over and saw my family and friends sitting across the court room, some of them were crying also. And some were just staring at me with a blank face, not knowing at all how to act.

This, I think, was the saddest day of my life. Not just because of my own loss, but because of the pain I was causing my loved ones. They loved and cared for me, and me for them. I knew that. I also knew I'd miss them, and I could deal with that. But what I couldn't deal with was the thought that they'd miss me too. That's what broke my heart.

Being in the courtroom that day seemed as if I was attending my own funeral. I could see that my loved ones were really going to miss me and that I was truly loved in my life.

It's a pretty strange feeling to stand there and watch yourself as if you're now dead. And as they all stood there mourning my passing, I wanted to yell out to them, "I'm still here! Don't be sad. I'm okay, and I love you guys too." But for some reason, I felt that my words wouldn't have been heard, as if I wasn't really there.

Just as the dead lay quiet in their coffin, waiting to be taken to the tomb and put to rest, I too was quiet and waiting. But I knew my tomb awaiting was not of peace and rest, but rather a tomb of restlessness. For I now knew my destiny. Today I would not be passing back through the door in which I came and into my old life. But rather through the door which leads into the tomb, this tomb of the living called prison.

I believe it's true what they say about a dying man and his thoughts. Right now, I'm not thinking about the money or the things I've got to do. Instead I'm drowning in the thoughts of unspent time with my loved ones. That's what it's come down to in the end. The people I loved and the time I wish I still had with them.

My life was a blink of an eye, and at this point in time, I'd do almost anything for just one more day with them. And if I like it or not, I'm having to face the big question of my life right now: Did I love in the pure sense? Or was it always just about me? The answer to this unwanted question is truly agonizing.

Well, I just got the bright flashlight in the eyes again. The guards do cell check every few hours and want to see your face. The shine of the light comes so quickly and strong that it's like a blinding slap in the face. I completely freeze almost every time it hits me.

What really gets me is that sometimes I'll be looking the guy right in the face as he peers through my door window, but still he shines it straight in my eyes. Man, that bugs me. I never seem to beat the draw of the light and turn away in time.

How does David sleep so well in here? If you're sound asleep and they don't see your face, they hit the door hard with their flashlight or kick it so it rattles the place. They want to see you move and know for sure that someone is still in there. So how do you ever learn to sleep through this?

I've noticed already that inmates in prison are more laid back than in the jail house. It's like they've accepted their lot and have settled into it. The jailhouse guys are still trying to beat the system and get clear of the big mess they're in.

It's like they're fish in a net. The net has closed on them, and they're flapping around, trying to get out. The net is pulled from the water, but they're still fighting. Not ready at all to accept what's happened to them.

Then it happens. They're out of breath. Realizing they're caught and going nowhere. In prison most guys have stopped fighting it. I'm starting to accept it myself, but it's going to take some time to get used to this life.

The difference between jail and prison is crime, time, and the line. A misdemeanor crime would be done in the jail house, and the time is usually under one year. Felons usually do more than one year, and they do that in the penitentiary. Though they do stay in the jail house until moved to the prison.

The line is the space of confinement. Jail is like living in one small room of your home, and you can't go outside. Prison is like living in your bathroom, but you can go outside and walk around the block. But do remember, it's not a nice neighborhood.

Jail is short term; prison is long term. And when I got here late this afternoon, I started noticing the differences right away. The guys in here carry themselves totally different than the jail house guys do. It's the difference between the way a major league baseball player would walk out onto the field, and the way a high school baseball player would walk out onto the field.

The body language tells it all. It's like when a lion walks, it doesn't second-guess itself. It knows what it is. The prison guys have that seasoned feel to them. They've been to war, and you see it on them. Their eyes say, "This is not a game, boys, and we're not playing around in here." It's the real deal. It's their home, and you've just come into it. And after a few tests and trials, it might be your home also.

Each man in here caries such a strong and distinct sense of power. You feel as if you were some small frightened child walking your way home through an unknown fairy tale land of angry ogres. And you can't help but ask yourself the question, Will I make it home?

The jail house is full of guys sticking their chests out, flapping their wings, and trying to look big and bad. In here no one is trying to look tough. You know right away that won't work in here. They know who you are already just from looking at you. I don't think you can hide who you are in here, no matter how hard you try. It's the law of the jungle, and everyone knows their place.

When this night is over, it will be my first full day on the yard. Today I got here kind of late, so I settled into my cell and took a shower. I sure don't like always having to wear shower shoes, but I guess it beats athlete's foot. After showering, I hung out close to my cell to get a feel for the place. David did show me around the prison yard a little bit. It was great to be out in the open air again.

This place is really pretty big, kind of like a little city of sorts. A city of criminals, that is. I have no idea what to expect out in the yard tomorrow. But I'm glad that my time has finally started, and I can get this whole thing behind me. And yes, I'm definitely a little scared of this whole prison thing. I've seen a few prison movies myself, and in a few hours, I'll know if they were really true.

THREE

I just heard my cell door unlock. They hit the switch from the control room at about 7:00 a.m. But you still need to hit the button yourself from inside to have the door open. That way, no one can just come into your cell. For your own safety.

The door is all steel and has a window on the right side of it. It's only about four inches wide, like the back two windows of the cell. It goes from about the door handle to the top of the door. The glass is pretty thick too, with wire net running through it.

I can see some guys heading for the kitchen, which is just outside my pod. It's across a little dirt courtyard. It sits on the edge of the dirt track, which is basically the yard. It's only about thirty feet away from my cell.

A pod is one group of cells. The pods are in the shape of a half square. The guards' control room is off to one side. My cell is almost all the way at the end of our pod. There are only two cells to my right side. At the last cell to my right, stairs lead down to the bottom tier and into the yard. To my left are more cells. At the end of my row, it corners around to another row of cells and the showers.

The guards are able see the cell doors and everything in the pod from their control room. But they can't see inside the cells or showers from there. The only way to see inside them is to walk down the row and look through the windows. The control room is where the guards can lock or unlock your cell. It's also their safe house from the inmates.

It kind of looks like the way a motel looks, if you're in the parking lot looking at the rooms (two stories high). It's the same setup. Except here, the parking lot is a dirt yard. And were the pool would be is the kitchen. And the motel office is the guard control room. There's also two sets of stairs on each side, but no ice machine.

The yard is a little bigger than a football field. There are pods all the way down the length of the yard, on one side only. There are about eight pods total. On the other side of the yard, there are the administration buildings and the entrance into the prison.

A dirt track goes around the entire outside of the yard. And the buildings all sit on the outside of the track. My pod is on the far right side of the yard when you're coming into the prison. At the far left of the yard is the hand ball court. In between the handball court and my pod, there are more pods. The kitchens, barbershops, laundry rooms, counselor offices, phones, and library are all spaced between the pods.

The phones are on the walls at the end of each pod. There are no incoming calls, just outgoing collect calls. On the inside of the track, there is a football/soccer field, weight pile, boxing ring, and the always busy basketball court.

Inmates can see the yard from their cells. Depending on where your pod is determines how much you'll see. My pod is too far down to see much of anything, just the corner of the track. Everything sits pretty close to the weight pile, which is about the halfway mark of the yard.

David says it's good that we're this far down the yard. The weight pile gets noisy and wild. Boom boxes playing loud and guys talking crap. And lots of fights.

The weight pile has a large net covering high over the top of it. This helps to keep the sun off you when you're working out. It's the only shade covering in the whole yard and a blind spot. A blind spot is where the guards cannot see an inmate from their control room or gun tower. They don't have too many blind spots in here, which I think is a good idea. People get hurt in blind spots.

Now try not to get too good of a picture of this place. When I say it's like a motel, it's far from that. It only has somewhat of the layout of one. The design must be for better inmate control.

If the prison has to regain control of the place, all they'd need to do is start at the administration building at the entrance of the prison and push the inmates across the yard and back to their cells. I've only been here for about fifteen hours, but I already know this place could get out of control in a heartbeat. There are rapists, murderers, child molesters, and some other pretty violent guys in here. This place is definitely a little crazy, to say the least.

On the bus coming here yesterday, this other fellow Mark and I were the only ones chained together, out of maybe forty of us. We had ankle chains, wrist chains, and our hands were chained to our waists. With all of that, they still had the both of us chained together.

I asked Mark, "Why do they have only you and I chained together?"

He said, "You've got me, Paul. What did you do?" His tone was like it was my fault, not blaming me outright, but like I was the bad guy out of the two of us.

So I told him about things getting a little crazy one night and that I happened to hurt a couple of guys in the process. Then I asked, "What'd you do, Mark?"

He said, "I got high and poured gas on my old lady and tried to light her on fire. I chased her down the street, trying to light the match, but thank God, it kept going out."

I played it real cool, but on the inside, I was freaking out! I knew right then Mark and I were not going to some little work camp prison. We were going to some big bad prison. Mark and I were both classified as violent and high-risk inmates. Before my talk with Mark, I thought maybe, just maybe, I'd be going to an easier prison than where I now knew I was going.

You see, they don't look at what happened at the crime or how the crime happened. They look at what you were charged with, your conviction. Armed robbery sounds pretty bad, right? Like someone put a gun in someone's face for money. But maybe what really happened was that the guy used his finger for a gun. Then he got away and got caught later. And the cops say they could not find the gun used, but the person who was robbed says he most defiantly had a gun. So he really did not endanger the victim as to shoot him, because there was no real gun involved. But the crime or charge is dangerous and violent. Now I'm not saying that's okay. The guy using his finger is a criminal, for sure. What I'm saying is, it's the charge that counts, not the circumstances, as to which prison you go to. At least in my case, that is.

The bus had all types of prisoners on it. And we were all heading to different prisons throughout the state. Some were easier than others, such as work camps, DUI camps, and minimum security units. And some of us were going to medium security units and maximum security units.

We were all coming from the same initial maximum security holding unit. This is the place that decides which prison you go to. They classify you depending on your risk to the public and your risk to the prison, and send you to the appropriate unit.

The guy I saw said I was a dangerous person, but he'd keep me close to my family. He wouldn't even let me say a word to him about my case. He just told me to stand there and keep my mouth shut. What a jerk, telling me I'm dangerous and to keep quiet and then saying, "I'll keep you as close as I can to your family," as if he was doing me a favor or something.

When I'm asked the question, it's always asked in the same way: "What are you down for?" They usually don't go any further than that. The answer can really be misleading. My charge is "attempted aggravated assault."

Some ask, "Who'd you beat up, and what'd you beat them with." I tell them, things got crazy one night and I hurt a couple of guys. I leave it at that. For the guys that just can't handle the mystery of my answer, I give them the highlights. I was driving drunk and got into a head-on crash.

The day it happened started out like most days. I woke up to this beautiful southwest winter weather. This time of year is especially enjoyable for me. After growing up in the Chicago area, my whole life I was extremely grateful to have blue skies and sunshine, while back home, they had gray skies and snow.

Anyway, I had some time and wanted to go see some friends that day. We all sat around talking and drinking coffee for most of the afternoon. After coming home, I took a swim and headed inside to clean-up for an evening out. Throughout the night, I stopped at a few bars. As always I had a great time drinking, dancing, and meeting new people.

It was well after midnight driving home. I stopped off at a drive-through to get a burger. I was only about two blocks from opening my front door and sliding into bed. I can still remember listening to the radio and changing it from song to song.

Suddenly, *wham!* My seatbelt held strong, but the impact thrust me into some kind of breathless slow-motion moment. Then just as quickly, my ears exploded as the crashing wave of sound rushed over me, throwing my head backward and completely disorienting me. I felt the weight of my car in complete resistance to something extremely powerful. My windshield was smashed in so I could see nothing but utter blackness. While hitting the brake pedal and grip-ing the steering wheel, I held on for my life. What was this huge surge of power stopping my car? I had no idea.

Now in the shadow of the hazy distant streetlight, I cautiously opened my car door. For a moment, things were very still and silent. Then one by one, porch lights started breaking through the darkness. The silence was interrupted by a few barking dogs and the voices of the neighborhood. I heard a soft moan coming from something still in the shadows. What I thought were to become my first steps of survival actually became my first steps into this nightmare. I could not believe what I saw.

I walked over to the man I heard moaning. He lay there in the street, now unconscious. I could hear another man in pain some dis-tances away and went over asking what I could do to help him. His leg was broken, and he couldn't get up. He said only one thing to me: "Go help my friend."

As I walked back to the unconscious man, I saw what looked to be like a motorcycle crunched up in the street.

Oh my god, head-on with a motorcycle! It was his head that hit my windshield! At that instant I realized what had happened and started screaming at the tops of my lungs. "Help, someone please help." Over and over, I screamed in a complete panic, pacing back and forth in the street. Some woman on her front porch yelled over to me, "I called 911! They're coming!" My heart sank deep inside my chest realizing I was totally helpless to help them. Not knowing what else to do, I sat down on the curb and waited.

Help arrived and took the two guys to the hospital. A police officer came over to me and gave me the whole DUI Test. To my amazement, I failed and was completely stunned to be arrested for the cause of this horrific car wreck.

I woke up that morning the good guy with a real life and went to bed that night (in jail) the bad guy, with no life.

They told me, "DUI is not the charge against you, not when you hurt someone. It's aggravated assault, and that's a felony."

It does not matter to the people hurt or to the court . . . if you're sorry or not sorry, where you come from, who you are, where you've been, where you're going, what color you are, good looking, not so good looking, rich upbringing, poor upbringing, how much money you've got, where you went to school or for how long, criminal record, no criminal record, have a good job, don't have a good job, retired, or just getting started. It does not matter one bit. The only thing that matters when people are hurt from drunk driving is how long of a prison term will be sufficient for your crime.

Let's say you, the reader, has had just a little too much to drink one night, just a little. You're a block from your home, but a cop pulls you over. You don't pass the DUI test and end up going to jail that night. Okay, you're pissed and you think you were driving fine and that they totally overreacted. You're not smashed out of your mind. But yes, you admit you had a little buzz going but really not that much of one.

Okay, now let's say the same exact thing happens to someone else one night, some nobody. They're driving home, and they've had just a little too much to drink, just a little now. And they're not smashed out of their mind either. But yes, they admit they have a little buzz going, but really not that much of one. But this time, there's no cop to stop them. And they don't happen to see your loved one out there. You know the one, the one you love more than life itself.

Well, they don't see them in time to stop, and they run right through them like they're not even there.

Now you're not going to say that the drink's had nothing to do with it, are you? You're going to say, "That ———. This wouldn't have happened if they were total sober." You're also going to tell the judge to lock up that no-good drunk and throw away the key. This was your loved one, and they need to pay for it. Right? So why do "we" think it's okay for "us" to drink and drive after just *a few harmless drinks*?

Drunk driving is one of the few crimes that is committed by an otherwise law-abiding citizen. When the drunk driver's brain wakes up, they can't believe they are a criminal. They have basically become a criminal in their sleep.

We need to choose not to drive after drinking, before we start drinking.

After a few drinks, almost everyone thinks they can drive well. But that's the tricky part of it. Your sleeping brain is the one talking, not your awake brain. And just like when our brain is asleep at night, we do things dreaming that when awake we really can't, or just wouldn't do.

FOUR

Well, they just made last call for breakfast on the yard loudspeaker. I sure hope it's good. The jail house food was awful. I just about starved in there, with the little-kid rations they gave us. We had bologna sandwiches on white bread, a spoonful of corn and maybe an apple, and always Kool-Aid to drink. It was never enough food to take away your hunger, but just enough to keep you alive.

Anyway, today's the big day. My first "wake up" here in the prison. I have no idea how it's all going to happen out there in the yard. I feel completely lost right now. It's like being in a totally different country, without knowing the customs or language. It's really kind of scary.

When I got here yesterday, they just kind of set me free, so to speak. I was not told the rules of the place, when or where I could go, or not go. They did not tell me what time to get up or what time lockdown was. They didn't tell me what time we eat or when I could shower or not shower. They tell you nothing at all when you get here. They just open the door and send you out into the prison. Today I have no idea what to do or what not to do.

When we drove up to the prison yesterday, the bus first stopped out in front of these very tall and powerful-looking prison gates. As we waited for the gate to open and let us in, I thought, *Oh my god, this place is freaking crazy. It's a fortress.* As the gate slowly slid close behind us, my only thought was, *Oh my god, I'm not getting out of here until they say so!*

When the bus finally came to a complete stop inside the gates, everyone on the bus stopped talking, and no one made even the slightest move. It was the moment we had all feared. It felt like forever as I listened to my own heartbeat, anticipating the pass from this realm of life into the unknown realm of prison life. It was that space in time between life and death. It felt like how it must feel taking in your last breath of life and wondering what's on the other side.

In a flash, we heard the guard yell, "Let's go!" as he opened the steel screen door that divided the inmates from the driver and shotgun man. The two guards walked us into the administration building single file while the guard in the gun tower and a handful of other guards watched nearby. There were about ten of us inmates walking into the building, and all of us were shuffling our feet with quick steps, to keep from tripping over our ankle chains. The only sound over the guard yelling "Move it!" were our chains jingling as they hit the ground. No one said a word, and our eyes were all beaming wide open. I think most of us new guys were in total shock.

I felt like a gladiator might have felt going into the arena before his first fight. I was completely engulfed with adrenaline as I looked around in fear, and awe, of this whole new world that now surrounded me.

When we got into the administration building, we walked down a very long and narrow hallway with its exposed plumbing high overhead. The dirty white walls had scuff marks and a few holes in them. I kind of got the feeling that maybe some of the other inmates at one time or another weren't real cooperative coming into the building.

The only thing that looked neat and clean was the newly painted shinny gray floor. We came into the inmate processing area, which was nothing more than the end of this long hallway with a few wooden benches up against the wall. There was a guard behind a glass window doing paperwork. The guard that we all followed through the door and down the hallway told us to sit down as he handed a file folder through a slot in the glass window to the guy sitting down.

The other guard that trailed behind us through the hallway to the benches immediately started taking off our ankle chains followed by our wrist and waist chains. It was a relief to finally be unchained from Mark and to have a little space of my own.

The two guards now seemed to be a lot more at ease than during the last few hours of our transport. Maybe it was because their job of getting us here to the prison was now over or maybe because we were now all so subdued and quiet.

After about ten minutes, our paperwork was done. Time to go to our cells. The guard said, "OK, guys, let's go" as he started walking into the sally port only a few feet from our bench. A sally port is the transition room between one secured area to the next. It's kind of like an airlock. You go in through a doorway into this small room with big thick windows on both sides. The door locks behind you and then the door on the opposite side unlocks and slides open to let you out into the other side. There is a guard behind the glass window that operates the doors. This is all so that no one can make it out of an area by going through only one door.

I assumed each of us would be escorted to our cells and was shocked when the steel door finally opened and only us inmates walked out to the other side.

The guard handed us each a small piece of paper with our cell number on it. He gave a quick glance out into the prison yard, saying, "Head that way, guys." He, of course, stayed safely inside the sally port. He acted like someone who just put their trash out to the street curb. He didn't even give us a second look back. And I'm thinking, *Why would he? We're the trash, right?*

As the solid steel door started to slowly close behind us, we all just looked at each other. It was as if we were all lined up and waiting to hear the starting gun of some race none of us wanted to race. With a loud, echoing bang, the sally port door finally closed. The race of our life had officially started. Though our eyes were moving at the speed of light, our feet were frozen still. No one moved. I felt like a steer might feel on his way down the narrow shute to the slaughter house.

While standing there at the edge of the prison yard, I momentarily sensed freedom. The view was overwhelming after being locked up inside that small dark cell. I was now gazing up at the clear and cloudless sky. My smile grew as each breath of warm desert air filled my lungs.

I've always loved the Arizona sunrise and sunset, and it had never once crossed my mind that they could be taken away. I had seen the sun once from inside the jail house. A few inmates and myself were let out of our cells for church service. We were all following the guard down a semi-long hallway to the jail chapel. None of us had seen the sun for some weeks now. As we turned the hallway corner, we were suddenly ambushed by the sun. It came beaming in through this long shoulder-high window so intensely that when the warmth of it hit our faces, we all stopped dead in our tracks.

We were up five floors from the ground, basking in the sun. Shielding my eyes and looking down, I was able to see part of the city. It was not the best part of town, but for some reason, it now held a sort of beauty to it. It's like we all at once remembered there's life out there. Real life. No one said a word, we just stood there motionless with our mouths wide open squinting through that big picture-like window.

Right then and there, I heard a soft whisper inside myself, "Always remember, it's the little things that are the big things."

Suddenly the guard started yelling, "Let's go! Keep moving, you guys. Come on, let's move it, now!" We didn't care what he said, and he could yell all he wanted to. We weren't moving yet. It was as if we didn't even hear him. Like someone was yelling at you in your sleep and you can hear them, but it's like they are far away and talking through a tunnel to you. It's all muffled and hazy sounding. We were all going to enjoy this moment for as long as we could, and we did. It was only for about thirty seconds or so, but it sure filled me up with a lot of hope. And maybe just a little sadness also.

I had forgotten there was a whole world out there still living. When you're stuck in a small room with no windows for a period of time, your world becomes very small.

Anyway, back to standing outside the sally port. The scary part comes as you look out onto the yard and realize you have to walk across the whole thing to get to your cell. That's when my stomach did a double flip and dropped. After a moment or two I said, "See ya later, Mark," and started walking in the direction of my cell. Mark headed off to my left toward his cell, which looked to be even farther away than mine.

The yard's pretty big, and I thought I'd never get there. The inmates just kind of look at you as you come walking in here. They don't yell anything rude like the jailhouse guys do. Maybe it's because you're both out in the open, and you can see each other. In the other place, the inmates were always behind cell doors when you came walking in down the row, and you couldn't see them through the glass window of their dark cell. They'd yell stuff like, "Put sweetie in here with me!" or "I want him over here!" In here, they just look at you as you walk in across the yard. So I did just like I did elsewhere: I kept walking, not looking for too long at anyone.

I felt the way it might feel to walk down Main Street in the middle of rush hour totally naked, with all eyes upon you. Or maybe the way a gold fish might feel stuck in that little plastic bag coming home from the pet shop. When he's dropped into the fish tank, he thinks he's free. But then suddenly, he realizes he's not free, and the other fish are not gold fish but piranha fish, and he's the meal.

It's like the whole prison sees you coming in. DOC makes that real easy because you still have on the jailhouse orange jumpsuit. Kind of like the gold fish. All the guys in the prison have prison clothes on—blue jeans, blue button-down shirts, or white T-shirts and then, here you come. It's like you're screaming out loud, "Hey, I'm the new fish!"

It didn't take long for me to find the cell door with the big B22 on it. I walked up the stairs to the second tier and passed by a couple of cells on the way to mine. I heard some very loud music coming from one of the cells I passed. At that moment, I realized I hadn't heard music in over a month.

It was amazing and almost frightful to feel the sound of music again. It's as if I was flat-lined on some hospital bed in the ER, dead as can be. As the doctor reaches for the paddles on the crash cart, he yells, "Clear!" and my body jumps from the zap of the paddles as my heart is shocked back to life. All at once, they look at the monitor, hoping to hear the *beep-beep*, as it shows life once again on that little red line bouncing across the screen.

It was pretty weird, to say the least, feeling that "life" inside me again. I didn't even know it had gone until it came back again.

As I looked through the window of my cell door, I saw this guy sleeping on the bottom bunk. The door was cracked open, but I knew better than to just open the door.

I'm really starting to live by instinct in here. It's like you just start knowing what the right thing to do is at the right time. In here, you don't want to get that wrong.

I knocked on the cell door and woke him up, saying, "Hey, I'm Paul. They told me this would be my cell also."

He jumped up off his bunk and opened the door all the way. "I'm David, come on in." He was real nice about it and seemed like an all-right guy.

It could have gone the other way just as easily. I've heard of convicts telling the new guy, "You need to find another cell. You can't stay here." I think at that point you'd better fight the good fight. I'm really glad it all started out well with us.

David said, "Let's go get your stuff."

"What stuff?"

"You know, your sheets, pillow, blanket, towels, soap, shampoo, and your clothes. You'll also need some boots. New guys get a whole bunch of stuff. Come on, let's go. I'll show you where."

Then as we were walking out of our cell, he stopped and said something real casually, like it was no big deal. It caught me off guard when he said, "Get ready, the AB will be up here pretty soon to give you a heart check."

"Who's the AB, and what's a heart check?"

"The Arian Brotherhood, ya know. The white boys, they'll be up here soon to kick your ass. They do it to all the new white boys when they come in. They want to see what you're made of."

I'm not sure why this came out of my mouth, but I said, "You go tell the AB that the first guy that comes through my cell door is going to get hurt."

Now, I didn't say this to try and sound like some kind of tough guy or anything like that. I didn't know who the AB were. I knew this place was for real though. So I needed to be real.

I started to think pretty hard about who I really was. I didn't want to hurt anyone or be hurt myself. I just want to be left alone and do my time and get the heck out of here. I'm not sure if he told them or not. But part of me hopes he did, and the other part hopes he didn't. Maybe they were just too busy yesterday to come up and see me. Maybe they'll come up today?

How do you tell who's friend or foe? David's seems all right and all, I guess. We do have to live together, so I think there's a real good motive to get along with each other. At least I hope so.

Being the new guy is always sort of hard. I want to fit in and get along, but that already seems like it can be kind of hard. I know I'll need help finding my way around and figuring out how things work in here. But I get the feeling that prison is not the best place to ask for help. Kindness is taken for weakness in here. From what I'm seeing, this is definitely the last place in the world someone wants to show weakness.

FIVE

Waking up in here today is really depressing. I have nothing but my haunted past running through my head. What can there possibly be for me to look forward to. God, help me through this day.

Out there I used to get up extra early just to watch the sun come up. I'd go out to my chilly, but always relaxing patio. It was surrounded by wet morning grass and tall beautiful orange trees. I can still remember how fresh they all smelled as I sat sipping my first coffee of the day.

It was just me in my sweats on that comfortable patio chair, barefoot, sitting and staring into the dark sky of the still and silent morning. As the sky slowly opened, night slipped away, and the soft deep blue of a new day was now shining through. Quickly united and never far behind, orange dusted with yellow, pink streaked with purple, and finally, life-giving red were brilliantly spilled out together across the canvas of the new morning sky. My spirit was alive.

As the sun rose, so did the birds; a few would start chirping softly at first, then louder and louder, singing their songs and moving in the trees. You couldn't much see them, but it seemed as if more and more awoke every minute. There must have been hundreds of them. I don't know, but it sure was peaceful and always so renewing for me. As if life just started all over again in that moment. It was *now*, and whatever was to come was going to be great! I would drink this deep into my soul, for I knew it was the hand of God . . . I thanked Him for another day.

Sunrises are always like that for me. Totally new. Like a kid that's never seen one before. At least they used to be that way. That's one more thing I don't get to have in here.

Just thinking about that makes my whole being thirsty for it again. God, do I wish I could have just one more drink of that.

It's taken about a month from my last court date to where I sit today. Two weeks in the jail and two weeks in the prison classification unit. And it doesn't take long to see that things in the locked-up world are rough, tough, and very unforgiving. Everything from the people you meet to the surroundings you live in. Even the clothes you wear are so starched and rigid that they're hard to walk in. Everything has that harsh, hard feel to it. You couldn't break something around here if you wanted to.

There's no carpeted floors, no soft chairs, no plastic toilet seats, no window coverings, no bathtub to soak in, or quiet time to relax in. There's no dogs to be petting or kids to hear laughing. There's nothing at all that even comes close to the free world. Even the inside air you breathe is thick, still, and hot, with the stench of unbathed bodies. There's no softness at all, just steel and concrete. Even the people's eyes have a hardness and a hate to them. It's the coldest, sickest place I've ever seen.

You're pretty much camping twenty-four hours a day in here. If you're cold, you'd better get to moving your body so you can warm up. If you're hot, you'd better put some water on yourself and lie down on your cell floor to cool off. If you're hungry, you'd better change your mind. If you're not feeling good, you'd better get tough and suck it up until it passes, because you're not going to get what you want, as fast as you need it, that's for sure.

It's as if you were out in the middle of nowhere. It would take some time to get back to civilization. You'd need to hang in there and take good care of yourself. Instinct for survival better kick in fast, or you're going to be meat for the wolves.

In here, it's just like that. Things take a long time. You need to learn how to take care of yourself until hopefully, you can get to some help, or it all just passes. One night I had no pillow, no blanket, no mattress, and no bed, just the cell floor. I thought it was a real blessing, though, to have a full roll of toilet paper. I used it as my pillow that night sleeping on the cold concrete floor.

I had no idea before prison how soft and comfortable my life really was.

Breakfast was actually pretty good today. They served scrambled eggs, sausage, toast with jam, apple sauce, and milk. The chow hall is set-up like a cafeteria. When you first walk in, you grab your plastic fork, knife, and spoon, then continue down the line. There's four guys dishing up the food, one scoop at a time, behind this glass window. They put a scoop of food on your plastic tray, then slide it down to the next guy, until it reaches you at the end of the line. There's a guard watching the whole process, making sure no one gets more or less than they should. This includes the one and only pint of milk per inmate, which is guarded like gold.

I've heard it said, the kitchen is the heart of the house. Well, prison is no different. It was kind of weird going into the chow hall just now. All these guys were sitting around, talking, laughing and acting like it was just another day in the good life.

As I walked in, I saw all kinds of people from all kinds of places, and I realized some of them probably never had it so good. I know that's messed up, and kind of heartbreaking, but very true.

I sat down in the white guy section, of course, and I didn't say too much at all. The tables hold four people with these round seats that come up off the table pedestal. It's all steel except for the seat itself. You straddle the seat because the steel bar that holds the seat up is between your legs. The tables and seats are hard plastic, and it's all bolted down to the concrete floor.

The chow hall is divided into separate sections—by the inmates, that is. On the far left side of the food line are the blacks. On the far right side are the Mexicans, and right in the middle are the whites. Some guys would stand by the side of the wall with their tray of food, waiting for someone to finish eating, so they could sit down in their "color" section. Even though there were plenty of open seats in a section that was not their "color." I saw no one cross the cultural line and sit with another color, only their own.

Although I pretty much kept to myself, I did acknowledge the guys at my table with a "How's it going?" Then I just sat there, eating my breakfast and looking around the place. I waited for them to first engage the conversation. This one guy at the table named Dave (a big Texas boy) asked if I just hit the yard. I told him I just came from Phoenix. I think his cell is to the right of mine. The other guys at my table were this kid named Mike and a guy named Louie. They all knew each other and seemed pretty friendly. We exchanged names, that's about it.

I did learn something new at breakfast from Dave today. When you are finished eating and get up from your table, you should, "out of respect," knock on the table—*knock, knock*—as you are about to get up. Just as you would normally say "Excuse me," when getting up from the table in the free world. He told me he thinks it all started back in the day when inmates were not allowed to talk at their meals but still wanted to be respectful to each other when getting up.

I actually felt exhilarated walking out of breakfast today. I was strong, healthy, and totally alert. It sure felt good to feel good again. My mind was clear, and I was completely ready for the day ahead. Maybe it was the real food? I had no idea I would feel like this in such a controlling and yet primitive environment. I'm sure glad I did, though, for I was about to walk into my first test and taste of prison life, and of course, when I least expected it.

I was born with the warrior's spirit. This is not a fighting spirit as you might think, but a warrior's spirit, and there is a definite difference. Even as a little boy, I knew I had it, but I didn't have a name for it then. There were many times in my life that I opposed my own spirit, and at the time, I thought I was embracing it. Things always went wrong when I did that. I now know that real warriors can walk away from fights. My oldest brother Steven taught me this. He has the warrior's spirit, and he embraces it.

I believe that the warrior's spirit is a kind and caring spirit. This warrior is a lover of all people and of life itself. He is even quite childlike. He is drawn into the battle through love—yes, love—not hate, and it's only within this realm of belief that the warrior's spirit

41

becomes such a fierce fighter. The warrior's spirit hopes not for war, but for peace.

I had decided to go to the library after breakfast and try to find something good to read. It's located on the second tier of the pod right next to mine. I didn't feel like going too far from home quit yet.

As I sat there reading and enjoying my solitude, two scruffy-looking convicts came strolling in. They were both unshaven and kind of dirty looking, not like they were out playing in the mud but more like they just didn't like to shower except every other Saturday of every other month. The younger of the two was in his early thirties and had on the typical blue prison beanie hat, blue jeans, and a gray sweat shirt. He also looked to be in pretty good shape. The other guy was dressed in old state-issued blue jeans with the typical blue button-down prison shirt. He was in about his midfifties and really fat. He moved like a walrus that had nowhere to go. They both looked and acted like they'd been in prison their whole life, strutting into the room with their prison-issued brown leather boots.

I thought nothing of it at first, being the only guy in there. The younger guy walked right over to where I was reading and grabbed a book off the shelf. He stopped short, only about four feet from my chair. My chair faced him as he faced the book shelf, and there was nothing between us but air. I kept looking at my book, acting like I didn't see him. He looked just like a convict you'd see in the movies. I really didn't think that much of it, until I looked over and saw the big guy standing in front of the door, blocking the only way out.

At that moment, my spirit awoke to what was really going on. I glanced up to the guy in front of me. He was slowly thumbing through a book and not even looking at it. He was looking right at me. When my eyes met his, he said, "Hey now" (prison ling-go for hello). I gave a nod back saying, "Hey," then looked back at my book, ignoring him.

He then put it all out there saying, "I like punks." I looked up from my book at him, not believing what I just heard. But I played it cool. My thought though was how badly I was about to hurt this guy.

He had no idea that his nose was about to break in so many places that it would never be the same. Or about how he was going to look out in the yard, laughing with the boys, missing his front teeth. I had no doubt in my mind he would wake up on the floor wondering where he was and what had happened. He'd have to ask big man, who'd also be lying there with him, holding his groin.

Body language told me the whole story. The guy telling me he wanted me was weak on the inside. I just knew that. And big man was a follower, not a leader. I think he would have held his ground at the door, but only because he wouldn't have known what to do next.

So after my thoughts of victory, I looked up at Mr. Rape Man and said (like I was happy for him), "All right." I then looked back at my book and kept reading. He didn't know what to do or what to say. I think he was stumped at my response to him. Or maybe he saw the pain coming his way? I don't know why, but he put his book back on the shelf and walked out with big man.

I knew it was time for me to get out of there. Who knows who might be up here next to tell me what they like. My first lesson was a good one. No place in prison is safe or sacred.

I think I'll start jogging again. I need to be able to have some time away from people and clear my head. On one hand, I feel totally alive and almost buzzed with the adrenaline, and then, on the other hand, I can't just turn it all off and go relax. In this heightened state of being, I feel almost primitive and pumped full of life. It's actually a pretty powerful feeling. This is life in the rawest form. Anyway, it's been almost two months since I've ran, and my spirit is really calling for it today.

I was so close seven months ago to a life with the good guys. I wanted to be a US Marine. The recruiter said there should be no problem with me making it. A reconnaissance man was my dream. All I needed was to take my physical, and that would have been a breeze. The week after my crash, I called the recruiter. He said he couldn't help me now, not until my charges were dropped and I was cleared.

One mistake and the dream dies, but regret lives forever. Don't trade your destiny for a day.

God, what a wasted life. I would have been a great soldier. Instead, I'm locked up and at war with my own countrymen.

I think I'll head for the barbershop. It's all the way down at the other end of the yard, but I'm ready to adventure out. I don't think I'll stay so close to my cell after knowing that things can go wrong anywhere. My hair is pretty short, but I want it all buzzed off. It's pretty thick and blond, and I don't need the looks, if ya know what I mean.

As I'm walking down this dusty track to the barbershop, I can't help but think about walking down the street to the Fourth Avenue barbershop in my hometown. That's where I'd get my haircut as a young boy, John's barbershop. I can still remember my mom almost every time sending me back to have more hair cut off. And of course, it was John's fault, not mine, that my hair was still too long. Mom sure would be proud of me now, going for a crew cut, all by myself.

The L-train station was there on fourth, which was the end of the line going north. Most dads in the neighborhood would take the train into Chicago for work, mine included.

There were a few other shops there also, like the hardware store, drug store, pizza parlor, deli grocery, and last but not least, Leo's newspaper stand. Leo's was in a small corner of the train station. It's iron gate with chain would be pulled all the way open early every morning. It was a poorly lit and musty corner of the train station and so very small that Leo even had merchandise hanging from the ceiling.

Leo's was mine and my brother's favorite store in town. We could get all the good stuff there—candy, comic books, ice cream, and even fireworks. Each time you went there, you'd see stuff you never saw before. You never knew what you might find on your next visit. We really loved that place.

Leo was an incredibly kind old man who always stood hunched over in the front corner of his store. He'd always take your money with a smile and a sincere "thank you." His worn-out bloodshot eyes were sad, but always gentle. You could see that life had been hard on him, but he still choose to be kind.

We all knew Leo's story—the town, that is—though we never talked about it with him. I think Leo knew that we knew. You see, Leo was a Nazi concentration camp survivor. His whole body told the story, but still, there he was, seven days a week with a smile. Leo had such a warmness about him that you'd always leave there feeling good about yourself.

We lived in Wilmette, Illinois, an all-American middle-class town, just north of Chicago. We were on the east side of town, only a few blocks from Lake Michigan and Gillison Park. Its boat harbor was full of private yachts and big sail boats. Wilmette had some of the nicest and cleanest beaches around. As kids, we'd spend most of our summer days at the beach, swimming or just riding our bikes. There were tennis courts, baseball fields, play grounds, and lots of green grass.

Wilmette was a town filled mostly with families raising their kids. It had some great schools, including New Trier High School East, which was in our school district. You were almost guaranteed to get into a great university after attending schools on the North Shore.

So where did I go so wrong to wind up here in the Arizona State Penitentiary, and not out there in the Arizona State University? I know it's my fault, but I'm not exactly sure how and where I went so wrong. But I do know this: I'll have plenty of time to think about it.

It's crazy, I fell into some comic book nightmare. Seeing this side of life is really mind blowing. Is this life real, or am I going to wake up any minute now? I sure do wonder sometimes.

Like right now, I'm walking down this prison yard track on my way to get a haircut from some convict who's going to be holding sharp scissors to my head from behind. And God only knows what he's in here for. I sure hope it wasn't anything to do with scissors.

Well, the haircut went just fine. I do look a little like a bulldog, but hey, it's prison, not Hollywood.

SIX

I just heard my name called on the yard loudspeaker; they want me to go up to the administration building. DOC seems to always be yelling something on that speaker.

They called me up there to say I'll begin working this afternoon on the chain gang. Everyone starts out working the chain gang, and after thirty days, you can "try" to get another job. There's about eight hundred guys on this yard and only so many jobs. I'd really like to be working in the kitchen. I know I wouldn't go to bed hungry working in there.

If you don't work, you go to the hole. I think I'll choose to work. It's only five days a week, four hours a day. Two hours in the morning after breakfast and two hours in the afternoon after lunch.

The pay is really pretty funny; it's five cents an hour. Yes, I said *five cents an hour*. I'll make *twenty cents* a day. Can you believe that! Well, if that's what it pays, then that's what it pays. At least I'll have some money coming in when my money runs out.

I gave my brother Steven a few grand to hold for me. He'll put it on my books as I need it. You can't have cash money in here; that's contraband and a guaranteed trip to the hole.

Working should also help pass the time. It seems like a lifetime ago since I've worked. And I do look forward to having a routine again. You can only lay around for so long before you start getting lazy.

Like my buddy Craig says, "All work pays the same." It took me about two years to figure out what the heck he meant by that. And what I finally got was, all work pays you . . . self-respect, self-esteem, self-confidence, self-worth, and a good night's rest.

In the heat of the day, it's about 100 to 110 degrees out there. I should be kind of used to it though. I've lived in Arizona for five years now. But then again, I always did have a swimming pool and AC to come home to.

Our cells do have air vents with swamp coolers. But it's really warm air and not much help for cooling down.

I've now been on the chain gang a little over a month. They call it the chain gang, but we don't actually wear chains. Though on our way to the work area, we do walk in two single file lines as if we were chained together. There's one guard walking with us on one side and another with a shotgun driving behind us in a truck.

The first day they walked us out here, I thought we were going to be worked to death. But it wasn't like that at all, it's been just the opposite. It's more of a game, or should I say, a mind game, than a job.

To anyone on the outside, it would look like we're really doing something worthwhile. We're on the outside of the yard but still inside the gates. What we're doing is filling a wheelbarrow full of sand and moving it about twenty feet away. Then we're spreading it over any low spots behind the cellblock walls. It's about as interesting as it sounds.

There's about thirty of us out here with shovels and rakes, and only one wheelbarrow. I've decided to make this job a challenge. I look at the work as a workout. Every day when the guard asks for someone to take the wheelbarrow, I jump at it. It's not like I've got to fight anyone for it, but I grab it before anyone else can.

It's not that pushing a wheelbarrow is fun or anything, but it's the standing around doing nothing that's boring me to tears. And I know I'll be moving if I've got the wheelbarrow. Only about five guys can fit around the wheelbarrow at any one time, and the rest of them just stand around watching the others shovel.

They'll fill the wheelbarrow as full as they can hoping that I spill it. And then I'll go as fast as I can trying not to spill it. They all look at me like I'm crazy and can't figure out why I'm in such a hurry. But I just half smile and laugh, as I'm running back to them, saying, "Come on, boys, give me some more."

It's a great workout. And remember, I'm getting five cents an hour. It's a double win.

Today the guard told me to sit down and be the water boy.

I passed out water cups for two hours. I think he's caught on to my little game. As they see it, we're out here to be punished, not to enjoy what we're doing.

Officer Harris, our boss, is a real hard nose kind of guy. He really hates convicts. All the guys hate him back. And they do all they can to get over on him. But I kind of like him.

He's a black guy in his midthirties. He reminds me of the drill sergeant in the movie *Officer and a Gentlemen*. He yells just about everything he says.

His clothes are creased, clean, and sharp, even in the heat of the day. He's got the look of a hardcore military man that could take care of business if he needed to. When he talks, he looks you dead in the eye, with the confidence of a real soldier. His body language says, "I'm in complete control here, guys, and you're not." There's not an ounce of fear on him.

After work, Officer Harris calls your prison number. You're supposed to come up to the front line and get your photo ID card. That's the procedure; they have to make sure all the inmates are accounted for. I still don't have my prison number memorized. And it's especially hard to hear it when he yells it so fast.

One day, I heard my name called out. When I got up front, he said, "Hey, you need to remember your number. That's who you are now."

I looked right at him and said, "Yes, sir."

Our eyes locked together without any movement. I realized no other inmates called him sir. I didn't say another word as he was trying to figure out if I was mocking him or truly being respectful. When he did realize it was respect, he handed me my card and said,

"See you tomorrow, Top Gun." So now he doesn't call me by name or by number, just Top Gun."

I found out through my cellmate, David, that some guys on the yard were asking if I was recently out of the military. They said I had that look and smell about me. I told him how close I came to getting in just before prison. And I'd be in the U.S. Marine Corps right now if it wasn't for my car crash. Maybe that's what they're smelling.

I've now become pretty focused, disciplined, and committed to changing what doesn't work in my life. I don't know what life after prison holds for me. I do know I'm going to fight like crazy to be all that I've been created to be. No more wasting time blowing in the wind, hoping my life will just all fall into place . . . if and when I ever leave this place and take a second swing at life. I'm going for a homerun this time. Like they say, "When you're on the bottom, there's no place to go but up." That's a great saying and all, but what I think needs to be said is, "You'd better build yourself a good ladder, or you're not going up anything."

The first time I saw this, I laughed so hard I just about fell over. Officer Harris stopped watching us so he could talk with the guard in the perimeter truck. As soon as he turned his back to us, all thirty of us guys stopped working. It was like watching a synchronized swimming routine. Everyone at the exact same time stopped working. I was the only guy that kept moving, until I saw what was happening and joined in with them. There are some harmless things you'd better do with the group than to go against the group.

We were raking sand at the time, and no one was going to give one more pull of their rake than he had too. As soon as Harris looked back, we all started working again, in complete unison. We didn't miss a beat. What made it so funny was that he took a double take. Harris knew what was going on, but he didn't actually see it.

It's now been a few months since I've been on the chain gang, and I'm finally starting to get into a routine.

Friday after work, Officer Harris called me up to get my ID card. When I got up there, he leaned toward me just a bit and said, "Hey, Top Gun, I've worked it out so that on Monday you'll start working in the kitchen." He handed me my work evaluation paper scored with the highest marks.

I was totally shocked and didn't know what to say. When I finally did speak up, all I could think to say was, "Thank you, sir."

He just smiled and gave me a nod. He knew that I admired him, and I think this was his way of saying thanks. He has to be tough or else these wild men would eat him alive.

Getting the new job really caught me off guard. It was only a few days ago that I asked the cop in our kitchen if there were any job openings. He told me he didn't think so and looked at me as if to say, "Yeah, good luck, kid. Get in line with the rest of them."

Whatever Officer Harris told him about me, I sure do appreciate it. Because from now on, I'm working in the kitchen! Whatever the work is, it won't be out in the sun pushing a wheelbarrow eating dust. But I will be eating a lot more food. No more going hungry in this house.

I'll be able to start working out hard. I'm going to get my running back up to par, along with some serious weight training. At the moment, I weigh about a hundred and seventy five pounds. At six feet tall, I need to get back to the two hundred pounds I was before prison. Maybe just a touch bigger this time.

Before this whole ordeal started, I was working out twice a day. Once in the morning and once at night. I'd also run for one hour every day. I loved doing this for almost four and a half years.

Some people have trouble keeping the weight off. I have trouble keeping the weight on. When I lift weights and run, I put on muscle. But if I stop, I'm back to nothing but skin and bones. We've all got are body challenges. And we all believe the other guys got it easier. I guess that's just human nature.

DOC just called a code red lockdown. It's only two-thirty in the afternoon; what could have happened? Eddy, the guy two cells down, just told me to get whatever I need. Code reds can last for days.

Everyone's running around crazy, trying to stock up on stuff for the lockdown. They're trading coffee, tobacco, and whatever they need. I'm stocked up for at least a week.

There's a guard on the yard loudspeaker yelling, "Code red lockdown! Code red lockdown! Get into your cells, and close your doors!" He's yelling as if there's a fire burning the place down.

My adrenaline is pumping pretty hard right now as I'm watching this all take place. I've got my foot up on the railing outside my cell door, acting like I don't hear the cop on the speaker. His eyes aren't on me anyway. I can see him through the control room window on the phone. He's standing up looking into yard.

Dave, my neighbor, just got back to the row. He's looking all freaked out, like he just saw a ghost. He said, "Some guy got all cut up in the yard. The guys' stomach was gashed open, and his face was cut to shreds with lots of blood. I saw two guys fighting and one had a razor. He was going crazy cutting the guy up."

A razor blade can be taken out of your shaving razor and put on the end of a toothbrush. You heat up the end of your toothbrush with a lighter and then stick the razor blade into it. Then cool it down in water. It seems to be one of the weapons of choice.

The guards will come and do a body check now. That's when they go from cell to cell, seeing who has blood on them, cut knuckles, or any fight marks on their body.

Until DOC figurers out why they were fighting and that no one else will start it up again, they won't let us out of our cells.

I've heard that even after the lockdown, it could go off even bigger.

The fight could've been racially motivated. If so, DOC will keep us locked down for days. They'll let the whole thing cool down before opening the yard again. If it is a racial thing, the guys are passing the word. And when our cell doors open again, the yard could have a war on it.

If this happens, almost anything can happen out there. If anyone's got a beef with someone, they could now choose to go after them. A lot of people could get hurt. And you never know who has something against you. I know it wasn't, but a few months before I came here, the yard went off. I heard it was pretty crazy.

When a few hundred guys are running around in every direction, it's hard for DOC to see who's hurting who. The only way to get the place under control is to bring in the goon squad.

The goon squad is a bunch of ape-like guards in riot gear. They'll come in here and put the pain on some people. Dave says, "If it happens, just stay in the cell with the door closed." I sure hope that's not the case in this situation.

Prison can be a little scary sometimes. Actually, most of the time. You just don't know what might happen next. It's always on-the-job training around here. It's not like DOC gives you a handbook on how to handle yourself as the goon squad comes rolling in for an ass kicking. You've got to learn as you go.

I guess I'm fortunate to have a neighbor to school me. Though it's probably to his own advantage to live next to a fish who's schooled, just in case something crazy goes down.

They call first year convicts a *fish*. It's because here in prison, you're a fish out of water. It's true, this is a world of its own.

Two guards just came to my cell door. Body check. They looked inside my cell window first. And told me to take off my shirt and turn around slowly. They came in and inspected my palms and knuckles for signs of violence. As they went off to the next cell down the row, I heard one of them joke about me not having any tattoos. My thought to them was, *My power's on the inside, pal.*

It's almost like I'm some kind of freak by not having any tattoos. Just about everyone has them. Some guys have more ink on them than the Sunday paper. I've already been asked by a few people why I don't have any. They always laugh a little nervously when I say, "They really won't look so good when I'm relaxing over in St. Thomas." They think I'm kidding. Someday, we'll see about that.

I also believe there's nothing manmade that's actually good enough to be permanently put on the human body. So I've never considered getting one.

We've been locked down all day now. It's eight o'clock at night, and regular lockdown is at nine. They now won't let us out until the morning. It really stinks sometimes being locked down. But then again, sometimes kind of nice being locked away from the craziness of the prison yard.

There are two ways you can look at lockdown. One way is you're locked away from the world and can't get out. The other way is the world is locked away from you and they can't get in. When I look at it as if I'm now safely locked away from the world, it's sort of peaceful and relaxing. A time to recenter myself and get ready for the next round.

SEVEN

Well, it's back to open yard this morning. They got the whole fight thing figured out and locked both of them down in the hole. It was a black and white thing. But nothing else should come from it.

The race tension is very real. Mike, the young guy I work out with, told me that some guys on the yard (white guys) don't appreciate me talking with Larry. Larry is a back guy I know from the weight pile. We've talked on the yard, and there's some people that don't like it.

We've talked about this with each other, and we both don't care what the others think. It's not like we're sitting with each other in the chow hall. Now that might be an issue with some people.

There's people I like, and people I don't like. It doesn't matter what color a person's eyes, hair, or skin is. To most guys, that's a big deal. But no one's giving me a hard time about it to my face. It's not like we're good hanging buds; we just talk sometimes.

I think they're still some white guys trying to figure out who I am. They see me on the track running for an hour every day and on the weight pile hitting it hard with Mike. But that's really all they know about me.

Now if the place went off, Larry and I both know what side we'd need to go to. But then again, I'm not fighting someone else's battle for them. It's really a gray line what I'm talking about here. Really gray.

The way I see it, the AB, the Blacks, and Mexicans all form groups with their own kind for the same reason. Safety. There's safety in numbers. People don't tend to pick on other people when they're a part of something bigger than just themselves. I don't condone or condemn these groups. That's just the way prison is.

David, my cellmate, is no longer in my cell. He was moved out about a week ago to county jail. He has to face some old charges. That means this cell is now mine. DOC sent some guys in shortly after he left, and they took out the top bunk. So now this cell is one out of maybe ten single cell bunks on the whole yard.

I have no idea why they did it, being that all the units are over-crowded. I'm sure not going to send in a kite. A "kite" is prison lingo for a "letter." The last unit I was in, there were five of us in a two-bunk cell. Two guys on the bunks and three of us with mattress on the floor.

It's so nice to have my own cell, my own space, and my own little hideaway. I know this is going to sound a little funny, but it feels like I just moved away from home, and I'm starting out on my own. It's a little scary, but great.

Dave was a great cellmate, but I'm happy he's gone. Living with another man in an eight-by-ten cell is like being in the car on a long road trip with a friend. You start out liking them, but by the time you arrive, you can hardly wait to get some space of your own.

My cell row is in many ways like any other neighborhood out there. There's people I know, and people I don't know. Some neighbors are nice to live by, and some neighbors make you want to move far away. There's no difference in that way here. In prison, your economic level doesn't dictate where you will live. We're all living in the ghetto inside prison.

A little about the guys here in my neighborhood. Starting to my right all the way down, that's two cells, is Eddy. He's your average Mexican American in his midthirties. You'd never guess he was a mobster, but he is. He seems to get along with just about everyone around here. He has three young kids, but they only come and visit him every few months. Eddy says that's not as much as he'd like, but his ex-wife doesn't want the kids around him. She says he's a bad influence and needs to grow up. He tries to joke about it all, but you can hear the pain in his voice when he talks about them. He's a funny guy that keeps a lot of people laughing around here, including me. But when he talks about the family he lost, you see nothing but sadness in him.

I think Eddy's got a good heart and could go a long way in life, if he didn't fall for the whole gangster theme. All he seems to think about is the quick cash and not all the broken hearts he's leaving behind. He acts as if there's no wrong in it, like it's all okay and there's no other road in life for him. But I see right through all that. He's dreaming of a real life, like the rest of us are. He just doesn't know how to get to it and thinks the shortcut is the only way to a life he sees everyone else living.

Eddy's even tried to convince me that the gangster's life is a good one. I've told him when I get out, I'm going for the simple life. He just laughs, but the look on his face says, "I wish I could do that too."

Most of the guys in here are not talking about having the simple life when they get out. They're talking about the next big score, the next big deal. The one that's going to change their lives forever. But from what I'm seeing, I don't think that ever happens.

The sad thing is, they're still trying to make it work, even in prison. No one is saying, "I should've stayed in school and studied my brains out, or worked hard and built a good business. Or joined the service." Instead I'm hearing, "I can make my life work without that crap. Who needs school, hard work, or the service."

"Well, you do" is my answer to them.

It's a false dream someone sold them long ago. And they just can't seem to say, "Hey, I was robbed. He sold me fool's gold." They've bought the big fat lie that promised a life full of riches and glory. This lie is diabolically disguised as the good life. There's more guys in here for their second or third time than there are guys for their first time, which proves, they're all trying to cash in on their "fool's gold." I think a new "X marks the spot" is what's needed.

There's so many "if only" thoughts that haunt me. And it really hurts my heart to look back at them. I've wasted so much time, precious time. We've got it made in this country of ours, with all its freedom and choices. There's really just about nothing we can't do or become if we put our mind to it.

Some people risk their very lives to come here to this land of opportunity. Most of us just don't get it. We just don't understand what the big deal is. Well, from inside this prison, I see what the big deal is. It's called freedom and the pursuit of happiness. Inside prison, there's no such deal.

There's one thing about coming to prison that I know beyond any shadow of a doubt. I choose to come here. My view of this is pretty clear from here. The road you're walking today will take you right where it goes. Period. I can't go south, if I'm on the road going north. Yeah, I know it sounds silly. To think you're going somewhere when you're not on the road that leads there, *that* is silly. The road I was walking on before prison started way back in my youth. This was a seemingly safe and smooth road until it slowly spiraled downward.

I didn't have any real meaning or purpose for my life. From in here, I can see that. But from out there, I thought my life would just come together somehow some way.

I can still remember being about four years old and watching my dad leave the house for work every day. He would kiss me good-bye, pick up his briefcase, and walk out the front door. I would run around to the living room window and wave good-bye. He confidently walked down the street holding that black leather briefcase on his way to the morning train. Nice memory. The point is I assumed that someday I too would have a black briefcase handed to me and my life would begin.

I believe all people are of value. But not all people feel that their lives will be of *a* value. The fact that I chose to drive drunk shows me that I never made a strong decision for the direction and meaning of my life.

Why would anyone who truly believes of their value hang it out there at the risk of losing it? The things we value are the things we protect. That's just the way we're built. If we truly valued the lives we're living and the meaning of them, we'd take care of them as we would a newborn baby.

You're walking down the street one day, and out of the blue, someone hands you a bag of money. Ten million dollars. What would you feel in that first moment? Wouldn't you feel totally elated knowing you were in possession of something of worth? This was going to change your life forever.

Would you swing that money bag over your shoulder and keep walking down the street? Would you risk all that money, thinking no one was going to rob you? I think most people would call a friend, a cab, or an armored truck to get safely home.

So why would anyone ever drink and drive, or even be a passenger? Why do we treat our own "precious and priceless" lives with less value than that of a money bag?

I think everyone knows the chance they take when choosing to drive after drinking. And maybe we've thought, "I'll be fine. It's not that far away. I'll make it home okay. I only had a few. Nothing's going to happen."

Like I was saying, we protect the things we value. If you really do value your life, don't come here to learn how to protect it. Protect it now while you've got a much better chance of keeping it safe.

Anyway, back to Eddy, his business was shipping. His crew went back and forth from the United States to Mexico. Big money, big risks, big prison time. I think he's still got about four more years to do, and he's already been here for over three years now. Eddy says he hired some high-dollar lawyer that kept him from getting the twenty years of time that he should have received. It was on some small technicality of the law and a lot of money that saved his butt.

Why do I talk with a guy like this? I think that part of the reason is I can see he and I have the same pain about our old lives. There's a piece of his heart that's a lot like mine. Like myself, he doesn't just miss his loved ones; he yearns for them.

Eddy and I always talk from our cell doors minutes before the nightly lockdown. He's also living in a single man cell. It's become a kind of ritual. We both stand at our cell doors, talking and waiting for that last call of "Lockdown. Everyone into your cells." We'll stand talking about our day or just laugh about something funny that's happened on the yard. It's a good way to end the day.

The last words spoken by Eddy each night are always the same: "Another day, brother." In which I'll reply, "Yep, another day, Eddy."

The tone of our voices here is as if we just pushed away from the dinner table after trying to eat an elephant. Today was only one small piece of this huge beast in front of us. And even though we know some of it is gone, we can't imagine the whole thing ever being completely eaten. But still here we are, chewing away at it, one bite at a time.

I think this ritual of us standing at the threshold of our cells is really more about us knowing what's about to happen. We'll soon be locked even deeper away from the world we used to live in. And what we want is the comfort of someone who knows and understands what's about to happen.

Being locked away throughout the night with nothing but your own battling thoughts is the core of prison life. This is the unspoken place of eternity for us all.

We know that outside, the night will slowly pass, but inside, this cell time will stand completely still. We'll hopefully dream in freedom, about that sweet day that never seems to come. And then once again, when morning dawns, we'll wake up to nothing more than this nightmare of an imprisoned life.

Nighttime lockdown is always bittersweet. Sweet, because I'm still alive with one less day to live in here. Bitter, because now the real battle begins. Again tonight, I'll fight the accusing thoughts of my past along with the fears of my future.

There's no escape from this fight. My thoughts from the past will come and tease me about what I should have and should not have done with my life before prison. And standing right next to the accuser will be fear itself screaming in my face, "You have no future after prison!" This is a battle I sometimes lose; it is a hard fight for me.

In prison, time does not exist. I know this is a hard one to grab, but it's very real for us. There is no such measurement here in prison. There's no beginning and no ending in this realm of space. There is only the moment, the same moment. It never starts, and it never ends; it's always just now. As if we stepped into some sort of dream land where the natural law of "beginning" and "end" has been suspended. Prison is totally unoccupied by time, just as eternity would be unoccupied by time.

Being in here is much more than horrible. There's still many more things I'd like to do in my life. And every day, I wonder if I'll get the chance to do them.

Back to some of the others up here. To the left of my cell is a guy called Crunch. He's a white guy in his late thirties. I've never seen so many tattoos on one man. He's recently tried walking away from the gang life. He's just too old to be playing the game anymore. He's been in prison most of his adult life. They don't seem to be real happy with the new direction he's taking. And getting out totally might just be impossible.

Crunch has been with them for many years and still has quit a bit of pull. Some of the other guys he's grown up with through the ranks do understand. But the younger ones think he's gone soft. I highly doubt any of them would say it to his face. His first name is Bruce, but he's been given the name Crunch for a good reason, I'm sure. With that said, I think it crosses his mind that they might think he's some kind of a punk now.

To be called "punk" is just about the worst thing you can be labeled with in prison. It can mean a few things, but mostly, it means you're a girly man in the real sense of the word or that you're weak and can be pushed around. Sometimes, you'll hear it said, like "He's been punked out." It's incredible how cruel people can be in this place.

Crunch has helped me in the understanding of prison life and how it all works. One thing he's told me is "Always be in check before you leave your cell." You've always got to be ready. I've been around the block a few times myself, but not in this neighborhood. I think it's smart to listen to someone who's been here a lot longer.

He seems to instinctively know who's for real and who's not. That's why we've been able to talk. He knows I'm also not into the yard games.

Crunch and I met when I was out on the chain gang. I heard this guy behind me talking with someone as we were out working in the dirt. Suddenly, a loud whisper was sent my way. "What sizes are those 501 jeans you're wearing?"

I quickly turned around. "Don't even think about it."

He just laughed. "I was just asking what size they were."

"Don't you worry about it. They're mine."

He said, "I thought you might want to trade something for them."

"Nope." And I walked away to work in another place.

I had my dad send me in some blue jeans soon after getting here. The state-issued ones are not a fun-wearing experience. They are messed up bad. One pant leg can be longer than the other, and the zipper might be sideways. Worst of all, the seam will ride up your backside for a real uncomfortable day.

Later, Crunch came over to where I was taking my break and introduced himself. "Hey, I didn't mean anything by that. I just hate these state-issued jeans and thought you might sell me a pair."

We started talking that day, and now it's carried into our cells. We both have the same unpopular goal in mind: to get out of prison without any trouble and have a real life once out. We talk mostly about the good things we hope to do someday.

I hope when I'm out, my "someday" will always be my today. Out there, I always said, "Someday, I'll do so and so." God what a joke that was. Now, in here, I *have to* say someday. When I was out there, I could have been saying "Today, today, today!" I'll never lie to myself again and put off today for a someday tomorrow.

Crunch is on my left, and Eddy is all the way down on my right. In between Eddy and myself are two big troublemakers, Dave and Jim. They're a couple of white guys in their late twenties. They're not the nicest guys on the block, but they could be the worst.

Jim is always going to the hole for not working. He says they can keep putting him in the hole all they want, but he's not going to work. Eventually, DOC will take him off the yard and put him in super max. By not working, Jim is disobeying a direct order, getting a written up each time. When they've had enough of him, DOC will ship him to super max. He'll be locked down 24-7.

Every time you get a write-up, you go in front of the board. The board (DOC) reviews the write-up and decides what your punishment is for the violation. Each inmate has a P&I score. The P is for public risk, and the I is for institutional risk. If you can't handle taking orders from DOC, your institutional risk score keeps going up until it's too high for this yard.

I think this yard is a 3 and 4 institutional risk score. Some inmates have come from max (5) down to this yard. Some have come from minimum (2) to this yard. I came from a max (5) unit to this high medium unit. If I don't get into any trouble, I could be down to minimum custody next year. But if I do get into trouble, I'll go up to maximum instead.

The thought of never leaving this place is a constant ache in my heart. There's a known fact here in prison: anything can happen at any time. I've never gone hunting before, so I've never killed anything. But if I had to, I am fully capable.

Jim's cellmate is Dave. He's another story and plays the convict game all too well. He puts on a good act in front of the staff, but he's really up to no good most of the time. You'd almost think you're on the street around Dave. He's too comfortable. He's a big Texas boy that walks around like he's back on the ranch. He seems as at ease, as if sitting on his front porch back home. Like they say, "you can take the boy off the farm, but you can't take the farm off the boy." That's Dave all right. He's going to act the way he always has, no matter where he's at.

Dave's also been in the Texas prison system. I guess he thought he'd give Arizona a try. Just a fast-talking convict with lots of long boring stories. I'm not sure what he's in prison for, and I wouldn't believe him if he told me anyway. There's some people you just can't trust. That's these two guys. They do seem perfect for each other. I think they'd sell you for a pack of smokes if they could get away with it.

This doesn't mean I don't talk with them. I do but as little as possible. Things seem to go smother when you're not outright rude to your neighbors. No matter how they're living. And like anywhere, it's about getting along with others. The only difference here is if two people don't get along, someone can get hurt. It's not like out in the free world where you can hide behind the law after you've wronged someone. It's prison law in here. And there's no place to hide. You'd be surprised how polite and respectful people can be under this law.

The ones that aren't minding their manners too well and play tough guy usually get a "tune-up" sooner or later. It's not like we're all walking around super nice to each other. But it's rather a man respecting man politeness that exists.

Anyway, to the left of Crunch's cell is a character of all characters. His name is TJ. The first time I saw TJ, I thought he'd just jumped off the movie set of some Mexican cowboy bandito movie.

TJ could be in his thirties or maybe even in his forties; it's pretty hard to tell with this guy. He's a four and a half foot tall Mexican American (more Mexican than American) with hair so long and a beard so thick and black that you scarcely see his mouth or frayed teeth.

You'll never get a good look at his eyes either because of the prison beanie that he wears pulled over his eyebrows. I have no idea how he can see peeking out from under it. He's practically swimming in his blue button-down prison shirt, which he keeps buttoned up to the top of his neck. His untucked shirt also hangs to his knees, covering his little but large belly. His kid-sized hands are usually hidden inside the long sleeves of his shirt. And none of this seems to bother TJ very much either.

He's a prankster and always messing with somebody's mind. He keeps himself pretty amused around here, playing jokes on people. Me included. Though he's a pain in the butt, you couldn't dislike him if you wanted to.

TJ has unknowingly taught me to always be on alert. Especially in your cell.

When I'm shaving in my little cell sink, I'll almost always leave the door open about a quarter of the way. It gets hot in this cave, and I like to feel the fresh air coming in when I can. TJ sees this as an opportunity to try and scare me, the fish. He tries crouching down below my door window and sneaking into my cell.

The door opens inward from the right, with the wall right next to it. I can see the door behind me through my four-inch shaving mirror over my sink. If someone tries to squeeze in past the wall and the door, I'll see them.

I've spun around and caught TJ each time he's attempted this, well before he's rounded the door. He thinks this is funny. And he knows I'm not amused by it one bit. This has kept me on guard every time I shave. I refuse to change my routine and close my door because of this little joker.

The other day as I'm shaving in my little mirror, I see my door start to slowly open. Except this time, I realize it's not TJ. No one would ever try to open my door that slow and just come in. As my door opens, I spin around with my fist drawn back. As soon as his face passes my door, I'm going to smash him.

Well, at the very last second, I see the DOC patch on the arm sleeve of this would-be bad guy. I had no idea how I was going to stop in time, but I did. Just in time.

I think God himself reached out and put the brakes on my punch. I could hardly believe that this fish guard had no idea what just happed. He was totally clueless to the fact that I was going to have to tell DOC that I just knocked out one of their own.

I'm sure that would have gone over well, as I'm standing in front of a judge with new assault charges. This idiot fish cop came strolling into my cell like he was on a Sunday walk. That almost cost me some more years of my life. Come on, dude, stay awake during training. It might just save your life, and my life too.

Anyway, back to TJ. I wonder sometimes if TJ even remembers half of the stuff he does? He's always high on heroin. Yes, you can get all the drugs you like inside prison. It's not a big secret or anything. They say it's always been this way.

How do they get it in? Yep, you guessed it all right. It's called keistering. From the word *keister*. Like in the phrase "get your keister out of here." Most of it comes in during visits. All I really know is that they put the drugs inside small balloons and bring in through visiting. When and how it all gets keistered, I couldn't tell you.

Because of the contraband, we all get strip-searched after each visit. As you might have guessed, this is a rather humiliating and degrading process.

After the visit, you're brought back into the strip search room. Sometimes, you're with ten other inmates, and sometimes you're by yourself. It's the same deal either way.

As the guard walks in, he puts on a new pair of rubber gloves. Some of the newer guards smile a little sideways as if they're some kind of doctor, snapping their gloves into place. The first time you see this, you can't help but think, "There's *no* way." And he's not. He's just messing with you. The gloves are used to keep the guards clean as they're touching your clothes and boots and any contraband they might find during the strip search.

The little smile that some of them give you says, "I'm in control here." And as always, we'll let them think so. But if you get down to it, we inmates outnumber them about one to one hundred on any given day. The ones that have been around a while know this and treat us accordingly. The others you read about in the papers.

After standing totally naked as your clothes are being turned inside out and thrown to the floor, you're asked to do some demoralizing things.

It's as if you've now become some lab specimen spilled out with the formaldehyde. You're just another cadaver at the mercy of the student who cares not for your name or the life you've lived. His only interest is the work at hand.

As you're facing the guard, he asks, "Run your fingers through your hair and around your ears. Okay, open your mouth and stick your tongue out. Now lift it up all the way and let me see under it. Okay now, arms straight up and let me see your armpits. Okay, good. Now let me see your hands. Palms up first and fingers spread apart. Okay now, palms down. Okay now, lift up your testicles. Okay, lift up your left foot and show me the bottom of it. Okay, good. Now spread the toes. Okay, now the same with the right foot. Last thing now, turn around bend over spreading your butt cheeks and cough. Okay, you're done get dressed."

This ordeal only takes about thirty seconds. And though it's a pain, it's well worth the visit.

EIGHT

The first time she came to see me I spent the night flooding my pillow with tears. Memories of her devoured me as I sank slowly into the night. I never did let her know, but seeing her again from inside of here just about broke me.

On the day Cindy was coming to see me, I became very nervous. I felt like an anxious child waiting for his birthday to arrive.

Cindy and I first met a little over a year ago at a dance with some friends. She caught my eye immediately as she was dancing to some fast music with a bunch of other pretty girls. She seemed so alive and playful, laughing and dancing with her girlfriends. An all-American girl with just a touch of tomboy in her. As I was standing there watching her dance, I couldn't help but feel as if I already knew her. The kid in me was coming to life, and I could hardly wait to go ask her if she could come out to play.

She and I became an "item" soon after that night and spent many fun-filled days together. But as always, I soon became restless.

She and I had said our last good-byes at the jail house after my sentencing. Neither one of us knew what might happen in our lives now that I owed the state four years of my life. So we agreed that we'd just wait and see what happens when I'm out. We were "on again off again" anyway before this whole ordeal had happened, so it was no big deal. Though we had strong feelings for each other, I think we knew that a prison relationship would be tough on the both of us. So we decided that being friends was a much easier way to go for now.

The paperwork she needed to fill out for visits took some time for DOC to process, so it had been several months since I'd last seen her. I didn't quite know how to feel about seeing her again from the inside of this place, though we had talked a few times on the phone and sent a couple of nice letters to each other also. But now, we would be face-to-face once again. And I didn't exactly know how I'd act with my now distant past right in front of me.

How will I handle seeing that smile of hers as she's walking toward me inside some pair of old faded blue jeans? I can already see that sunshine hair of hers washing down over her shoulders and falling past her waist. I'll really have to be strong and keep my composure when her eyes start searching for mine. If she breaks through and sees my pain, I might never stop crying.

There is nothing on earth more calming to a wounded man than the sincere compassion of a woman.

Our visit went pretty good today. I let her (and myself) think all was well and that my time was going just fine. I think she knew better but let it all go just the same. I couldn't help but notice the chilling of my heart since I've been in here. It's as if she was some kind of barometer for my inner soul, and I could see the gauge and the actual size of the storm that's been brewing inside me. Sitting with her today was like a cool swim on a scorching summer day.

Prison is the only real world I now know. It is all I know. Everything else is but a fading memory of a once upon a time peaceful dream.

I've had plenty of visits inside this prison now. I've had guy friends, girlfriends, brothers, and even my dad flew out from Chicago once to see me in this place. And you know what? They're always the same. A *dream*.

As your loved one pierces this realm of slow motion living, it always hits you how much they just don't fit into this place of harshness and pain. And that makes senses and all. It's just in the seeing of how different our worlds really are that blows me away. Like night and day different, like asleep and awake different.

When you enter this tomb of the living, we softly float into a dream. To us you are a dream, a wonderful dream. In here we live in black and white; it's cold and without contrast. While out there, you live continuously in warm brilliant colors. We feel this energy of life all around you, beaming from inside you. You softly invade the darkness of life we know to be true. It's as if a hole in heaven has opened above you; it shines right through you and into the faces of darkness and despair.

This is always a wonderful and life-giving experience. It is the breath of life to the living dead.

But then as in all dreams, we must reluctantly pass back into the world we live, expecting all of its days of perplexed uncertainty to be eagerly awaiting.

Most people know how it feels to have had a loved one pass away. It's a fairly long and painful experience going through the grieving process. It helps a lot to think about knowing you'll see them someday in heaven. Those feelings are very similar when you come here to live in prison. You know they're out there somewhere, and someday you're going to be with them again. But for now, we'll just have to wait and learn how to live without them.

Like most people, my heart has many scars. Some are old but not forgotten; others are tender and still gently healing. If you look close enough, you can see the pain behind every smile in here.

After every visit from the world outside, my heart bleeds again. The cut is small but always deep to the core. At our last glance, we smile sadly, wavering once more, just before my fist clenches in pain out of sight as they drift away once again.

It's too easy to get stuck in the grieving process. So after a few drops of sadness and vulnerability run down my chest, I stop the bleeding. Anger is a great tourniquet for sorrow. No one could possibly be angrier at me than myself, and it's pretty hard to feel anything else when your anger is hot and alive.

By our own selfish actions, we've completely wiped out our families from our daily lives. To think for too long about the ones you've abandoned and how you can never make that right again is a mind-torturing experience.

Well, there it is again, the flashlight in the eyes! Man, you just never seem to get used to that. You get lost in thought or in doing something like writing or reading, and then you hear a little something outside your cell . . . And *wham*, there it is! Before you even have a chance to think, it's the guard doing cell check. It's in the eyes once again. The night guards sure are a sneaky bunch.

I'm not sure which one startles me more: being awake and suddenly ready to fight when the light catches me off guard, or sound asleep not knowing where I'm at when the light awakens me with its long solid stare. Either way, it's a constant reminder of the life you're living.

Visits are the best thing that can happen to you in here. No day is happier, and no night is more sorrowful than that of visiting day.

As long as I'm talking about visits, my old cell mate, David, was full of it. His whole idea about the AB coming up for a butt kicking visit was bull. He should have said the white boys if anything. I've come to find out the AB is so much more than that. They are the true power in here and don't play games like that.

I've been in here for about a year, and what I can tell you is, I mind my own business, so they don't mind my business. Get it?

Working in the kitchen is a great way to keep healthy. I'm about 225 lbs now and getting bigger daily. I eat enough food each day to keep a full-grown horse alive. I work-out two times a day on the weight pile and run two hours a day on the dusty dirt track.

I've become an even better power house than before I missed out on the Marines. I've really blown up with all the workout time I've had. It feels great but also like a waste. Being this healthy and not able to use it, dang. It could've been used for the protection and safety of my country. Instead, it's for keeping other prisoners at bay.

In prison, anybody can be overpowered. Mostly, it comes down to this . . . Why try to bulldog the marine-looking guy with all the good stuff when you can take from the weak all the same good stuff and have no resistance.

Five guys have a good chance at taking my stuff, this is true. It's also true that, after the fact, I would go after each one of them as I saw opportunity to do so. And you know what? They know this about me. They've been watching me, just as I've been watching them. We watch each other in here, like animals watch each other in the wild. It's as if we're all at the watering hole, trying to get a cool drink without being ambushed and killed.

Consciously or subconsciously, we are always looking for the weak and for the strong. You must always know who is who and what is what. Remember what I said before. This is the law of the jungle here, and you can't hide who and what you are.

I have a pretty good routine. And I am very disciplined in this way of life. I allow for some event changes if need be, but I almost always get workouts into my day.

As I said I'm running for two hours every day. And this has been lifesaving. I look forward to it like nothing else in my day. It took a little time to build my running up. Running is a time of true freedom for me. I love being out there in the heat of the day, sometimes 100 degrees plus, as the sun heals my body from head to toe.

When I first broke through the two-hour mark, I thought I wouldn't make it. I was elated when I pushed through and conquered it. The first hour is the tightest, but soon after, you feel no pain. It's like you're floating inside your own world.

This is meditation in motion. As I shut the world out quieting the constant noises, my spirit comes to life. I step into this realm, embracing my spirit as I would an old friend, as he embraces me back in the same way. He always comes strengthening me, speaking good things about me and the adventures of a life to come. He tells me of the good life awaiting after prison. And always reminds me of the good I live in now, even in this very moment locked up. I still have life; I still have love.

I almost never want to stop at the two-hour mark, though I know I need to. Anything more would take away from my muscle growth. That's too important for me. I listen closely and give my body what it needs. I live in a war zone, so I need to be combat ready at all times.

I love my days of running. I hope they never leave me. Out there, you're totally free. Free from all distractions, free from people, free from negativity, free from depression, free from stresses, free from hopelessness, free from fears, and most of all, free to be me. My hopes. My dreams. My life.

NINE

I'm not afraid of dying inside this place, at least not as much as spending my whole life here. With only a few years to the gate, I'm what some consider a "short timer." And some guys really resent short timers.

There's always a chance of getting drawn into a situation that could set you up for more time. I've known of a couple guys that it's happened to. This is my biggest fear.

When I first saw his face peer into my cell, I knew one of two things was about to happen. It was going to be him, or it was going to be me. My adrenaline told me even before my heart could double beat that one of us was about to get hurt. I was sitting on my bunk when his anger shot through the window just outside my cell door. He caught me somewhat off guard because I thought this whole thing was settled when it all started.

I've never been the "let's take it outside" kind of a guy. If it's going to happen, then it should happen then and there. This crazy game of "meet me behind the school at 3:00 p.m." I've never understood. To me, that's pride fighting, not real fighting.

He had all the chances in the world to come at me in the chow hall in front of everyone, but he chose not to. And so then, why now? As he was looking inside at me and waiting for me to open the door, I sensed just a touch of hesitation on his part. I think his boys put him up to it. And like me, he really doesn't want this all to go down. But like I said, pride fighting.

No matter how much a person has ever deserved my brutality, I have never felt good for doing what needed to be done.

I moved quickly toward the door, not for his sake, but to show confidence and assurance that I was the one in control here. In a split second, I stood there, both terrified but fearless. Facing him straight on as I opened the door letting him into my cell. He closed the door slowly behind himself, never taking his eyes off mine.

Sometimes life shows up with death riding on its back. I sure hope he's not planning on dismounting in here today.

The arena crowd came to a roaring hush as the noise of the steel door finally reached its locking plate. For I now knew that life and death both were always only but a breath away. The whole world was watching, but no one was there.

As I stood there in boots, bare chest, and blue jeans, I knew exactly what this battle would be for . . . My wife I've yet to marry, my kids I've yet to see born, and my life I've yet to live.

I won't let him take this away from me or from those in my future. I'll fight fiercely for the love of these things but never again for the hate of another person.

The warrior comes, emotionally, mentally, physically, and spiritually prepared.

The man facing me today is totally blind to the destiny that awaits him. He unknowingly already lives in defeat.

For the battle is not won on the battlefield, but on the training field.

It was early afternoon on this slow and easy Saturday. The sun was out strong and bright so the yard was fairly quiet. Most inmates were hanging out in their cells, staying cool, and waiting for a visit. Except for a few guys on the weight pile and the loudspeaker calling inmates up for visits, there was not much movement. As the sun lifted high above our building, all shadows slowly disappeared. Only soft whispers of light now floated into my cell. Like the dusk of a warm summer night, all was still but yet so very alive.

I immediately broke the silence with, "So what's up?"

He looked at me as hard as he could and said, "You disrespected me, Holmes" (Holmes is like "dude" in prison language). I noticed he had one hand in his coat pocket and that he must have a shank by the way he's holding it there.

My first thought was, *No way, he does not have a weapon in there*. I realized no one would bluff such a thing in prison. We were on my turf, and for all he knew, I had a weapon of my own. A bluff was impossible. This guy really did have a shank and was obviously ready to put holes in me. God, what a crazy place. I somehow stayed calm as my mind's eye quickly showed me the way out. Though my way was as inhumane as his, it would be my way to victory. I saw it clearly. I slowed my breathing and waited for him to make his move.

He was about a half foot taller than myself and moved much slower than he knew. I would side step backward, blocking his knife arm, and then fall him like a tree. His large head would be aiming straight for the steel toilet bowl with all the force of a redwood. If the first hit didn't knock him out cold, then I would continue what I started until it did.

I already saw myself dragging his limp and bloody body from my cell and onto the tier outside the door. I would not have even tried to start and hide what I had done to this man, being that he came to me for blood, not I to him. He had left me no choice; my hands would be clean in this matter. That's the way I saw this deal going down, and it was only a moment away. I was ready, but scared. This makes me the hero of my own life. Scared, but still pushing through the challenge.

And if I would also confront fear for your life, then that makes me the hero of your life. This is why I wanted to be a U.S. Marine. It's what I value. My country and its people.

Anyway, here I am, waiting for this guy to try and put holes in me, when he says, "Hey, man, why'd you yell at me?"

Here was my chance to speak the truth. "You took those milks I had set up there for my bros. They were for them, not you. And you knew they were not yours to take. Yeah, I yelled over at you as you were walking away. How else was I going to get your attention? And you wouldn't have stopped and thrown them back if you thought they were yours to keep. You're right, I shouldn't have yelled at you in front of everyone. And you shouldn't have taken the milks. So as far as I'm concerned, this whole thing is over with. Unless you don't think so and still want some of me?"

He momentarily looked puzzled as he thought of my words. I don't think anybody's spoken to him like that before. At first, he didn't know how to quite take it. As air bursts from a balloon, so also did the tension within my cell. He spoke much softer now. "It's all cool, Holmes."

I replied, "Good, we're all cool then."

The only thing I did here today was speak the truth. I was wrong, and he too was wrong. And that was okay with the both of us. We didn't need to knock each other's brains out over this.

I know some guys are thinking I should have battled with him anyway, to be a real man and all. What a joke that is. Why would I hurt someone that was not yet "committed" to hurting me? That would make me a real coward, not a real man.

As he's leaving my cell, I glance out onto the yard. Now seeing the soft blue skyline just off the horizon, I smile. It was a good day to battle, but it was an even better day for peace.

Back on my bunk again, I think I'll just kick it here for the rest of the afternoon. I kind of need a little downtime after all that drama.

I can't help but wonder how one night of drinking got me all this. The life I live now is all because of one night! I got into my car drunk, and here I am. Sometimes this thought is just too much to hold on to. And then again, sometimes this thought is just too much to let go of.

TEN

The first time I remember meeting Him, I must have been about five years old. The summer afternoon was overflowing like honey, and it was dripping everywhere. The sky hung there so brilliantly blue and deep, you could have fallen into it forever. Only occasional puffs of snowy white clouds slowly drifted on by as I gazed upward in awe.

My sanctuary laid within the far end of the backyard. Sitting cross-legged in my summer shorts and white T-shirt, I could feel the freshly cut grass tickling my legs and the hot July sun caressing my crew cut hair and neck. A warm gentle breeze danced joyfully around me, inviting me to stay in the splendor of the day. This too was a place without time.

I could barely hear my mom off in the distance. She was in the kitchen with the sliding glass door open.

Thick shimmering bushes stood within my boarders like giant castle walls, giving solitude to the kingdom. I was eager for the day I would explore outside of them, all by myself. As for now, my only exploration was the kingdom within.

Though I really couldn't say from where, I somehow knew Him and He knew me. We had meet somewhere before. There were no walls built around my heart yet, and no guards at the gate. So I opened the door even wider.

Imperfectly perfect. I held no hate; I held no fear. Nothing blocked His voice of greetings and Grace. "I am at the King's table," He whispered invitingly. "Come join us."

I can't remember having any fear, hate, or judgment the day I sat at His table. That would come later in life, wrapping itself around my heart and smothering the faith, love, and mercy I had once walked in.

Some years have passed since that day of unspeakable joy. Unspeakable, because no words can even come close to the glory of it all. It's hard to believe, but until recently, I had forgotten all about that wonderful day of my youth, when He showed up for me in the place without time.

Well, here comes the guard for cell count. I hear his keys jingling as he's coming up the stairs to our tier. It's pretty late, but my light is still on, so he won't need to shine his flashlight in here tonight. I'm always up late writing on weekends. He'll quickly peek into my cell as he's moving on down the row, and I know for sure he won't get to the end of the cells and down the other stairs without at least one woken inmate yelling obscenities at him.

Sometimes during the late-night count, I'll stand at the door looking out my window. With my arms over head leaning on the cold steel door and my nose pressed up against the glass window, I'll stare out into the stillness of the empty prison yard. It's eerily silent out there in the dead of night. The bright security lights of the prison circle the perimeter. And like a closed stage curtain, the blackness of the night lies just beyond the fence line. If you listen closely, you can hear the night breathing quietly behind the curtain of darkness.

I usually don't say a word as I watch the guard pass by. Even though they hold the keys that keep us securely locked away, you can still feel their fear as they swiftly move past these human cages and back to the safety of their control room.

When you're consistently treated as an unpredictable beast and continuously caged like a zoo animal, you naturally become very raw and dangerous.

For a Saturday night, it was extremely quiet and almost suspiciously still. Most weekend nights are loud and alive. With all the TVs, radios, guys yelling from cell to cell, odd smells drifting from the air vents, and guards roaming around trying to keep it all together. It can get pretty crazy around here some nights. But not this night.

For within this night of lingering emptiness, there settled a bold and mysterious anticipation. Just as the unexplored jungle awaits for those who would courageously dare to enter, I knew this night of the unknown was waiting patiently for me.

Life before prison was a real fairy tale for me. I'd spend just about every weekend and even some weeknights out dancing the night away. I was a real superhero, flying in and out of people's lives till the dawn would break. I'd step from the morning shadows as the day shined bright, as if I were an ordinary man living a mild-mannered life. It was one of the wildest chapters of my life, and I thought it would last forever.

But then, it happened one day. My cape was lost in the wash. Like a sock that comes up mysteriously missing, it seems to have vanished into thin air. So for now, all flights have been canceled, and my feet are firmly on the ground.

Slowly my life fades, such anguish . . . Slowly your life fades, such anguish . . . From green, to gold, to the ground are the seasons of life but never the seasons of love.

I've been locked in this prison cell all night, every night, for almost a year now. Tonight my spirit is overwhelmed with my youth. Locked up or not, this is still my life, and tonight I feel like dancing. Really it's more of a war dance that I'm feeling.

I've been thinking about this for some time now, but my embarrassment kept telling me I'd look foolish if I dared (even though no one would be able see me). Fear kept winning the battle, but not this night.

My spirit is growing stronger now that I'm spending time with Him. It's become a relationship of different relationships.

I'll need to back up a bit to make this clear. Long ago before prison, I was talking with my best bud about this whole God thing. I asked him how he knew who God really was. And his answer to me was quite simple: "Why don't you ask Him who He is?"

What a concept! No one has ever suggested that to me before. People have always said to me, "This is who He is." And everyone thinks they're right. So my thought was, *He'd show me if I truly wanted to know Him.* And so every night, with all my heart, I'd ask Him to show me who He really was.

I can't remember how long I was asking, but before I knew it, the answer was loud and clear.

As He embraced me, He said, "It's really good to see you, my friend." He smiled with complete sincerity as if He was saying, "Welcome home. We've been waiting for you at the table, ever since you got up and left."

In a day's time, I'll call Him many different names. For instance, Father God, Brother, Dad, King, Creator, Holy Spirit, Great Warrior, and Lord. He has many more names, but mostly, I'll call Him "Friend." He's the same God always. It helps me to be able to relate to him in different ways when I use His different names. So that's why it's a relationship of different relationships.

I can sense Him within this prison tonight. His stillness floats invisibly as if a thick fog down an old cobblestone street in the deep of the night. Tonight He's come for the dance.

It was another hot summer night as I sat on my bunk in the dark looking out the back window of this prison cell. With my bare feet up on the steel desk and my back leaning up against the cool concrete wall, I took a long breath and settled in. The music whispered softly throughout my cell as I stared off into the night. I was mesmerized once again by the rows and rows of razor wire that twinkled through the night.

There are quite a few lights outside the back of our cells. Powerful lights beam down over the cellblocks, illuminating the landscape and fences. As bright as it may be out there, the lights never shine directly into the back windows of our cells. Now the front of our cells (the yard side) is a different story.

Each night, the yard lights shine into my cell through the door window. It always shines in the same spot, tall and hazy, casting deep shadows within this place. The light lays softly and undefined on the wall right inside my door. It holds there steady, but it's filtered and fragmented through the distance it travels. It's about as bright as an old street corner light, so even in the dead of night, it's never completely dark inside this prison cell of mine.

Some nights are much lonelier than others. Being encased each night within this lonely tomb often brings my thoughts back to the days I knew. I'd lay awake on a long summer's night, lonely and alone, wondering how to get home, to my place that's still unknown, but aches deep within my bones. What will this life unfold to be, and will I truly, truly get to be me?

Lonely is lonely, and a tomb is a tomb. Though they're many different flavors, it all still tastes the same.

Suddenly, I felt as if I'd just pulled the safety bar down on some amusement park ride and was waiting for it to begin.

The stone has rolled from the tomb. As I am rising to my feet, I reach for the radio. Turning the key that withholds its freedom, I send it off, singing far beyond these walls. Feeling the freedom, I lift my hands high above my head reaching for the stars as if my prison cell was no longer there. Only, the open night skies and all its wonders hung over me. I remembered the heavens were still above, no matter where I was. And I could see vividly, within my mind's eye, the millions upon millions of stars that sparkled twinkled and shined mysteriously in the universe.

As it pours smoothly into my ears; the eyes of my spirit slowly open. It moves me, taking my hand as we journey. Teasing me with an overflowing of what I'm looking for, but never filling me completely. Promising me friendship, and bonding in our pain. We are both reaching in . . . the music.

In humility and grace, He walks right through the gates. When the breath of the lion roars, it's as a wave rolling through my very core.

I bathe in the nucleus of this new life, for He cleanses my tainted soul tonight. Sharpening my dull spirit for the fight, the strength of His solace shines from the stars all night.

As lighting strikes and thunder rumbles, I danced the warrior's dance of war and worship. Worshiping the Creator throughout the night is quite a profound experience.

When the dawn amazingly broke and the colors of life awoke, I stood with arms held high, grateful to be alive. Exhausted and yet exhilarated, I thanked Him for a night of . . . life.

When I finally looked at the clock, I could hardly believe how late it was. It was morning. Somehow I had danced through the night. I'd completely lost track of time or maybe time had lost track of me. Either way, it was once again, "a place without time."

Here's a story I've been thinking about . . .

Once upon a time, there were these two fish. They loved swimming in the ocean every day, having a good old time being fish. They would do this, that, and the other, all day long, every day. They also thought themselves to be pretty smart fish down in the fish world. They had acquired "the good life" that most fish dream of having.

So one day, as they're swimming around, living the good fish life, the one fish says to the other fish, "So what do ya think is up there in the sky of this ocean?"

The other fish says, "I believe there's nothing up there but more water at the top of the ocean sky. What else could there be?"

"Hmm," says the other fish, "I believe there must be more beyond this ocean sky. There has to be."

Well," the other fish says, "I'd have to see it to believe it. And hey, look! That worm hanging up there in the ocean sky, where did that come from? I'm starving."

The moral of the story? I wonder if God's angels ever look at us humans the way we look at the fish of the ocean. The fish don't seem to know there's a whole other world above them, and some people don't seem to know there's a whole other world above them.

In past circles, I've heard people talk about the "spiritual part" of life. Talking about the spiritual part of life is like talking about the "wet part" of the water. It's all wet, and it's all spiritual.

Anyway, I'm going to try and nap before breakfast is called. I've got a long prison day in front of me.

As I'm slipping off to sleep, I'm thinking about my little blue jean girl Cindy. She almost always comes to me in my dreams. Walking toward me from around the corner of some building, she appears. As always, she's joyful and full of life. Usually I see her beautiful bright smile long before I see anything else. Her soul piercing eyes twinkle at me with such delight that I stumble walking toward her like a nervous young boy at his first dance. I need to remind myself to breathe when seeing her intoxicating silky hair, as both sunshine and shadows trade kisses on her head.

She always walks right up to me, taking my hand into hers, fingers intertwined, as my heart races. She smiles and walks me right outside the gates as they open before us. As she's leading me to freedom in more ways than one, I feel her love completely engulf me. And the weight and hate of this place all falls off my shoulders and by the wayside.

We stroll down an old country road hand in hand, on a gentle summer's day. At the river's edge, we find a small shade tree with some soft grass and a few wild flowers close by. I hand her a flower with a smile. Breathing it in deeply, she smiles back at me while placing her forehead against mine and looking long into my eyes. She knows I love her, and I know she loves me.

Hearing the slow-moving river rippling against the rocks, and seeing the cool water roll on past as we sit inseparable arm in arm, is just about as heavenly as this earth can be.

ELEVEN

Well, it's back to routine. It's all about routine for me in here. My days in prison have now become just another life on planet earth. They are pretty much the same daily.

I wake up at 6:00 a.m. and heat my mini crock pot with water to have my coffee, freeze dried of course. I drink it black now and only for one reason do I do that. A guy in here can always get his black coffee, breakfast, lunch, and dinner. And you can also order/buy a bag of freeze dried once a week from commissary. But a guy in here cannot always get his cream and sugar.

The way I see it is like this: DOC almost always finds a way to take something else away from you. For example, one day you might have yard time, and the next day you might not. One day you might have the mail coming in, and the next day you might not. One day you might have shower time, and the next day you might not. One day you might have cream and sugar, and the next day you might not. But they always give you black coffee.

I figure the less I can live with, the less they can take away. So now, I drink my coffee black. Even when I get cream and sugar, I don't use it. I trade it.

After drinking coffee and reading my books that help center myself for the day, I head for breakfast.

They hit the cell lock at 7:00 a.m. when breakfast starts. It ends around 8:00 a.m. I'm not in a big hurry to get there with the first wave of people. Some guys practically run to the chow hall for their meals, as if they're going to run out of food.

After breakfast, I walk the track a few laps before heading back to my cell for another coffee and hopefully some quiet time.

Then it's time for a quick cell cleaning. Sweep floor, wipe down sink and toilet, make the bed, and mop the floor. All depending on the day of the week and how clean it is.

Afterward I'll either get a morning workout in as well as my afternoon one or hit the showers and clean up for work.

I work the lunch and dinner meals in the chow hall, so my mornings are all free.

My job is fairly easy. My buddy Mike and I work cleaning trays off after people are done eating. They bring their trays up to our window, and we spray them off with water and load them in the dishwasher. We are also responsible for scrubbing all the pots and pans that were used for the meal.

We actually have fun working in there. We listen to music, tell stories, and laugh like we're not even there.

Once, Mike didn't feel like scrubbing these cookie sheets we needed to clean. There were maybe twenty-five of them. They had burnt bacon on all of them, which is very hard to clean off. It was a Friday night, and the boxing match was going to start before we would be done working that night. On some Friday nights, there are boxing matches in the prison yard boxing ring.

Mike asked me to lookout for the kitchen guard as he opened the back door and slipped outside to the trash Dumpster. That would not have normally been such a big deal, because we were allowed to go outside with the trash to the Dumpster.

But this time, Mike had those dirty cookie sheets with him as he quietly lifted the Dumpster lid and dropped them in. He walked back inside the door smiling like nothing had happened. The cookie sheets would never be missed because the kitchen shelves were full with them. I was laughing so hard I had to grab onto the countertop to keep from falling over.

Mike started to wipe down the dishwasher as he yelled to the kitchen guard, "we're all done here, see ya tomorrow boss" The guard yelled back, "okay guy's, see ya tomorrow." Mike and I were already half out the door and on our way to watch some crazy prison boxing match.

If D.O.C. ever finds out what happened, we'll be in serious trouble. I'm one of the few people I know that's been here for close to a year, without a write up. I'd like to keep it that way.

Yep, we have some fun in there for sure. Best of all, we eat all that we want. Not bad for prison, not bad for prison at all.

Now I've seen it all. Absolute delusion of the masses. Tonight at the boxing match, Mike and I were at the very back of the crowd. There must have been three hundred men circled around the boxing ring. They were packed together tight as could be. Getting closer was out of the question.

We arrived as round 1 was close to ending. As the bell rang and the boxers went staggering to their corners for a quick patch up and pep talk. Mike and I repositioned ourselves for a better view.

Shortly before the bell rang for the start of the next round, the crowd suddenly erupted altogether. The roar was of pure pleasure. Only untamed testosterone could rumble the very ground under our feet as it did.

What did we miss? What happened? What's going on? We had no idea, Mike and I. And we kept our eyes glued to the ring, not wanting to miss whatever was going on.

In a million years, I would have never guessed what I was about to see. If you've ever watched a boxing match, you'd know that before each new round begins, a pretty girl walks around the ring holding a big card with the round number on it, showing the crowd the round that's about to start.

Well, being that there are no pretty girls in prison to do such a job, the inmates putting on the fight thought they'd find the next best thing. The next best thing for these guys is a well-known guy named Peaches.

Anyway, as I looked up, I saw Peaches in the ring walking with the big round two card. He looked as close as he possibly could to being one of those real ring girls. He even had on a self-made bikini and red Kool-Aid for his lipstick.

Being that the weight pile was pretty desolate, I told Mike "See ya" and headed for a workout.

After all the laughing is done, I feel the sorrow floating back to the top again. It's never completely gone. It just gets pushed down for a little minute.

Moving daily inside your sorrow is like trudging through thick mud in boots two sizes too big. Your legs are heavy with every failure, loss, and regret that you can't seem to leave behind yet. Sometimes this load is too much to bear throughout the long moments of a day.

I walk amongst failure. Every person that is here with me has a failed life. Everyone.

If you're "out there" reading this, you may say to yourself, "I too have a failed life." You might also be feeling knocked down, trod upon, and tired. You may be thinking your life is completely over and there's no hope. It's a done deal. It will *never* change or be the same, so what's the use anyway.

Well, the truth is, it's *not* over yet. I know it feels like it's over, but it's only really a season. A dark winter season for sure, but only a season, for sure.

And as in all seasons, they *do* change. I will not give up and sit down in the snow of this storm. I will walk day and night fighting for each step, until I reach the end of this horrific blizzard that now surrounds me.

The storms of life have tried to stop my journey many times. I will not be fooled anymore. I know the sun is somewhere high above these dark gray clouds that hover above me. The sunshine will in time break through. And the cold of the storm will finally melt away, quenching the thirst of this long journey endured. Victory will live.

Winter conceals the summer deep within her, just as an expectant mother holds her child deep within her womb. And only for a season does the sunshine of the newborn's face hide from the world outside. It's only for a season that the eyes of the newborn's life cannot see the wonders of this new life that eagerly awaits out of sight.

Then you'll hear the cry; your new season has finally arrived. As you look for the first time, you'll break down and cry. This new bundle of joy is now yours to hold, and I know you'll never want to let it go.

There it is again! The guard is doing night count, and every night he just has to shine that light into my face. Oh well, I know it's only for a season. I'm sure of that.

Like I was saying before, it's all about routine for me. Nights are my relaxation time. I absolutely love the cool fresh evening air. I think it's my favorite part of the day here. On most days, I've given it my all. Workout, work, eating right, chores, and minding my own business. Being out of my cell before lockdown and breathing the night air is a real treat for me.

Every evening after dinner, I'll walk the track. Most times myself, but sometimes with another inmate. Walking is a great way to start up a conversation. That's probably one of the best ways to get to know someone. We'll tend to pick up the conversation from night to night where we left off. You start knowing how well a person is doing their time after a few nights of walking.

Nine o'clock is lockdown. Our nights out are not long at all. Most of the guys are pretty much doing the same as always—walking, shooting hoops, handball, or a last workout on the weight pile before lockdown. Weeknights are fairly quiet in the way of drug deals and fights. It's pretty friendly out there most nights.

Once I'm back into my cell for the night, I might have a coffee and write a letter. Or maybe read an old one from someone that was kind enough to send one.

Some nights I'll just turn on my TV and get lost in a movie. Most guys have a TV or their cellmate will own one, so just about every cell has one. Commercials are pretty strange to watch because things in the free world are always changing. We don't get to see the changes except through the TV screen.

I'd say about 75 percent of my day has to do with athletics in one way or another. Walking, running, lifting, pushups, pull ups, sit ups, or handball keeps me moving and in shape for whatever might happen, and I truly enjoy all of it.

I'm really looking forward to making it to a minimum security unit sometime this year. I hear its laidback and relaxed at most of the minimum units. I've had no write-ups and some good work scores this first year, so I should hopefully be classified for a lower security unit at my next P&I risk evaluation (Public & Institutional).

Craps anyone? Pretty fun game actually.

Would you ever roll the dice for your freedom? I didn't think so either. When I decided to get into my car after all that drinking, I truly rolled the dice for my freedom and for my life. Think about it . . . I knew the odds. We all know the odds. God, what's the chance. And I won't lie, it wasn't the first time I rolled the dice on my life.

If I would've known that the last roll was for the whole dang pot, I would've picked up my chips and called it a night.

I can't stop from thinking about how that crazy night all came to pass . . . If I'd hit one more red light or one more green light. If I'd stayed out a little longer or maybe if I'd come home a little earlier. Or if, if, if. There's a million different "ifs" that could of happened another way that night. Then maybe this nightmare with all involved could have, should have, or would have never happened at all.

But you know what? The one thing I did have the power to choose was to get into the car or to not get into the car. That was the question. And I chose to do differently than what I knew was right. The key that turned my car engine on that night also became the key that opened this prison cell door, welcoming me inside.

If I would have just held that car key up high in the backdrop of the night sky, looking at it dead in the eye, I would've said, "This could be the key that also locks your prison cell door if you choose to use it tonight once more."

For most people (like yourself), a prison cell should be 100 percent nonexistent within your lifetime. It will never appear within the realm of your life possibilities.

Simply a fact . . . If you choose to drive when drinking, you choose for your 100 percent nonexistent prison cell to now be 100 percent existent. It has now materialized into the realm of good possibilities. In this very moment, a cold and lonely prison cell awaits for its next life to hold.

Looking back, I would've thrown those keys into the ditch that night and ran for home like a little boy with a skinned knee.

I wonder how many people this very minute hold a dual-purpose key like mine and don't even know it? Who will roll the dice tonight?

I'm not sure how old this prison is. But I know I am not the first person to live here in this cell. I sense that long after I am gone from this prison, years from now, there will be another person living in cell B-22 just as I do today. It's a very sad and surreal thought knowing this. I will be old and gray, and someone else will be living this life I now live.

Could this be true for some other things in my past life? Is there someone out there right now who's just recently graduated high school and awaits their journey? Are they looking at the starting line of life and getting ready to go? Wow, a little scary. But exciting. On your mark, get set . . . *go*!

They will stay out late tonight, as they hold tight to their youth in flight. Walking the shoreline will be a delight; will they go left or will they go right? All the decisions are theirs tonight.

Before prison, the days of life seemed to go on forever. It was as if I had all the time in the world to just sit back and slowly unwrap the gifts of this life. But as I sit here now, much older, I can't believe how fast those presents of the past actually vanished. My first twenty-five years of life flashed past like a childhood Christmas vacation.

I lived a whole lifetime before coming here to prison, and all I have left are a few fading memories in the far corner of my mind. And now, the life I lived is dead and buried. It's also unfortunately soon to be forgotten.

Why was I in such a big hurry for my life to happen? No matter what chapter of life I was in, I couldn't wait to get to the next.

There I was, racing to turn the next page of my life and missing the moment I lived in. I was running from the present moment by always dreaming of the next moment. Life was always right there in front of me. But I just couldn't see it.

Then one day from inside here, of all places, I realized something about my life. The prize I'd been looking for all along was right there in front of me, in the moment . . .

The prize is in the moment, and the moment is in the prize.

TWELVE

Late Sunday afternoon and visits are coming to an end. I didn't get one today, though I thought I might. It's kind of hard, but I try not to get too excited about someone coming. They can always fall through for any number of reasons.

It's always pretty depressing to expect a visit and then not get one. Actually, it's a hundred times worse than depressing and a fairly easy recipe that almost anyone can follow . . . Just add your two-pound bag of premixed fear and shame along with one cup of regret and a pinch of homesickness, and stir. Fold ingredients gently into your bowl of freshly picked abandonment and spread entire contents evenly into an eight by ten. Place in an 85 degree preheated prison cell and bake for one hour or until completely hopeless.

Once again you realize, deep in your soul, there's nothing in life that can ever be 100 percent there for you. Except the Creator.

I just heard my name called on the yard loudspeaker; they want me to report to the control room.

Wow, I can hardly believe it! The guard at control just told me to go roll my things up and handed me two cardboard boxes. After dinner, he'll come to my cell and inventory my things. Sometime within the next twelve to twenty-four hours, I'll be shipped out to a minimum security unit. For security reasons, they don't tell you when or where. From what I know, it will be between 2:00 a.m. and 4:00 a.m. when it's still and silent.

The guard said my papers came today. My P&I score has been lowered. They don't need the inmate there at the board to lower or raise it. I'll call everyone and let them know and have them pass the word along.

For a year now day after day, I've lived with the same eight hundred or so men, and guards. Most of the guys I get along with. Some I don't even know are here, and they don't know I'm here either. We pass each other, never acknowledging one another in any way. And then there are the chosen few, the ones I really don't like at all. And after tonight, I'll leave them all behind.

For instance, there's a sergeant (whose name I won't say) who is a real hater of inmates. No one likes him, including other guards. He's just plain old mean. I think he's always mad because he knows he was born stupid, but who knows.

I asked him a really simple question a few weeks ago, and he was a total jerk about it. He even had the guts to push out his chest and get in my face when he was talking with me.

Last week when I was doing my afternoon run, guess who shows up walking the track with a new female guard? That's right, Mr. Tough Guy Sergeant. I couldn't believe the nerve of this guy. He was in the yard like he owned it, struttin' and showing off the female guard out in the open. He's thinking they're safe because he's the sergeant.

There are only a few woman guards that work this prison, and they work mostly at night when the inmates are all safely locked down. Never do you see one on the yard.

We all knew what he was saying to us inmates by walking around the track with her. If they only knew the danger they were really in, I think it would have never happened. He was walking and talking with her like they were strolling through the park. Remember, there are convicts doing decades of time in here. And inmates outnumber the guards about one hundred to one on any given day.

Wouldn't you know it, I happen to be out running the track that afternoon. And when I'm coming around the last corner into the straightaway, I can't believe what I'm seeing. The sergeant and his pretty protégé are on the outside lanes of the track walking and talking like inmates are not even there.

To say I was mad is an understatement. It was as if someone was walking through the poor starving city streets of the Great Depression pushing a delicious-smelling hotdog cart while yelling, "Hotdogs! Get your red hot hotdogs!" And he knows there's not enough money between you and all your buddies to buy even a bite of one!

As I'm turning the corner, I put the speed on full blast. They are only about fifty yards from me when I hit the top of my sprint and drift over to their lane. My stride is about seven feet at this point, and only seconds away from them. I ask myself, *Why am I doing this?* I get no answer back. It's all primitive at this stage; that's why I can't answer the question.

As I'm heading for the bull's-eye like an arrow that's been commissioned, I know I've got him. By the time he hears me, it will have been too late. He has made a grave and fatal mistake . . . distraction.

He never even saw it coming as I blew past him in half a heartbeat. I felt him jump out of his skin as the tidal wave of fear rushed over his back and through his hair. I had to rethink if I'd actually brushed his shoulder sleeve as I kept on blazing down the track like a runaway locomotive.

Touching him would have been serious assault charge. The truth is, I don't know how I missed him as close as I came. He needed to know he's not as safe out here as he thinks.

I kept waiting to hear him or another guard yell stop, but it never came. By the time I finished the lap I was on and got back to that side of the track, they both had vanished from the yard. He can play it cool if he wants to, but he knows why I did it. I feel for certain he won't look at me the same again.

You, like myself, might be wondering why a guy like me is acting out so aggressively and all. Running past the sergeant in a flash of spite was a dangerous move on my part, that's for sure. Sometimes it's a hard line to walk. Show too much kindness and you're weak; show too much aggression and you're standing out too strong. Either one of these can get you in trouble, and I mean on-both-sides-of-the-fence trouble.

I'm sure someone saw the sergeant in my face that day up at the administration building. And I'm also sure that someone saw me out on the yard coming up his backside like a lightning bolt. The tone has been recalibrated. I probably wouldn't do it again, but I'm glad I did.

I'm just a man trying to live within this prison without this prison trying live within me. That's a one-day-at-a-time fight that most guys eventually just give up on.

It's as if the very walls of this prison are trying to squeeze that last bit of old life out of you. It grabs you firmly from behind and breathes calmly into your ear with a whispering smile, "This is for your own good."

After dinner, the word was out about my rolling up tonight. Mike and a few others came by to wish me well as I was going through my stuff and boxing it. I gave Mike an extra Bible of mine and told him he should read it. He knows it's helped me and has seen how I live. I also had a plant in my cell which will need some love. The plant was always considered contraband, but the guards would overlook it because I was not a troublemaker to them or others.

It's amazing to think that I've lived one whole year now with only two boxes of belongings. Out in the free world, I have a storage shed with everything of mine that's left from the old life. I thought that after losing everything and winding up with only a storage shed full of things, I had nothing left at all.

It's really pretty crazy in a couple different ways . . . I have lived just fine for the last year with only two boxes of possessions. And at the moment, I couldn't exactly tell you what I own out in that storage shed. Through there was a time before my crash that I had five times more stuff than what's in there now. And to think I used to believe it was all so very important.

There seems to be a lot of things from my past that I thought were very important at the time. Right now I can't remember why I ever thought some of them were even worth my time.

When looking back at my high school days, I thought four years was too long of a time for high school and not that important for me anyway. But now years later, with a four-year prison sentence hanging over my head, I see how important high school actually was. I wish I would have taken advantage of it a little more than I did. I know I could have tried harder.

Wow, that was really hard to say out loud. Regrets like that can sting. Knowing you are wrong within your own head is one thing, but speaking it out loud is a totally different deal. It actually takes muscles to do that. The freedom comes alive in the deliberate decibels, not in silent syllables held hostage within your head.

High school is the kindergarten of life. It sets the stage for your first act in the real world.

It's funny, I thought I had "arrived" when I reached high school. When in reality, I was still on the launching pad waiting to take off. High school is the launching pad of life. It holds you strong and steady while preparing you for the long journey ahead. Then one day, before you know it, you're ready to blast off into your new and exciting world of the unknown. High school, taken seriously and enjoyed, can be some of the greatest times in a young astronaut's life.

Tomorrow when I awake, the third long-distance bus ride of my life awaits. If it were not for the last two rides, I wouldn't be wondering if some new challenges might not be far behind.

The first long-distance bus ride I ever took was the one from Chicago to here in Arizona. When stepping up onto the Trailways bus one early Chicago morning, the words printed on the open bus door clearly called to me, "Watch your step." For little did I know, it was a warning for the new life I was now choosing to walk into.

I had decided to leave Chicago in the month of October just as the Midwestern fall was reaching its maturity. My sweetheart of two years had left months earlier for her first year of college at Kansas University.

It was fall all right, and the season of harvest could be seen everywhere, but the fall of my heart was kept hidden deep beneath the changing colors of the ambience and was seen by no one.

When the last of the leaves fell in whispers to the ground and the wind blew quietly with a much softer sound, I stood bare and alone, disbelieving that our time together was now gone.

As the days became shorter and the nights became longer, my tainted heart grew distant and darker. Now in a world without color, the sweetness of life had gone bitter.

Though Debbie and I had talked about how college was the best move for her, it was not for me. Though it was a real mirror for the condition my life. I was going nowhere fast, really fast. As I watched my three brothers, sister, and friends all go off to college one by one, I knew it would never be an option for me.

No matter how badly I wished to go off to college, I was not going. As I said earlier, I went to some of the best schools in this great land of ours. And I had some really good teachers to help guide me. And who cared about my education. So why not college for myself, you might ask.

The thing was this: I was what they called learning disabled, dyslexic. They said I saw letters and words backward. (Mean they what know don't still I.)

School was just a dream for me. I really enjoyed learning, but I just couldn't keep up in class for the life of me. I became frustrated with school. I remember thinking that if I could ever learn like the rest of the kids learned, I would learn *everything*!

I guess we all have our own challenges in life to overcome.

School was out for me, and life was not looking so good at the moment. Debbie's dad is a world renowned anesthesiologist and was always a really nice guy to me, even though I know I was his "nightmare" when it came to his daughter. And I get that. I knew that education was important to him and her mom. They both seemed extremely happy when Debbie decided she would go off to college that year, and not just hang out in the hometown shadows wasting her life away with me.

Though I loved her so, it was love that let her go.

After my girlfriend had left for her new and exciting life at school, I had no idea what I should do next. I had also been recently fired from my job, which was the icing on the cake.

The owner of the restaurant fired me from my assistant manager position. That would have been okay as far as jobs go. But Sam also happened to be my best friend, which really made it a little awkward.

I was not keeping up my part of the deal, so I understood completely. He and I remained friends for years after.

How could my world be so desperate and disappointing at such a young age? I had become a prisoner within my own life.

After a few months in the dark dungeon of depression, I tunneled my way out and escaped westward. My oldest brother, Steven, was attending school at Arizona State University and said I could come visit anytime. It was about a three-day bus ride. I had plenty to think about as we rolled farther and farther from the only place I'd ever called home.

I had no idea what Arizona held for me, but at this point, I was open to just about anything. I needed a completely new beginning. A do-over. Why not? Why can't we just start over in life, if that's what's called for. Just pick up and go. Start over.

It was a long lonely ride chasing the sunset. Day and night we rode. Most of the time, the bus was quiet. Unhappy people don't tend to talk very much. The only thing making noise was the constant humming of the bus engine, which could be felt throughout the bus.

It only took a few hours of riding that first night, and I knew I was on the wrong choice of transport. I wished I could've upgraded to a three-hour ride by air versus this three-day ride by dirt. But then again I knew I'd get some real quality time to think by way of bus.

I would try settling in for the long nights ahead by using my leather jacket as a pillow against the cold glass window. Though most of the time, I'd awake soon after slipping off to sleep, freezing in my T-shirt and needing to put my jacket back on again. Sometimes I would just lean my head forward on the seat back in front of me and drift off dreaming for a bit, until the pain in my neck and shoulders would nudge me awake. I would do this back-and-forth routine for most of the night. Finding peace only in short spurts of sleep.

Throughout the days, I would just lean back in my seat and watch the ever-changing landscape drift on past. Momentarily I would forget everything. Then like a bored child in the backseat of a long trip, the question would come at me once again. (And no, it wasn't "Are we there yet?")

It never seemed to care much for the "right time" when it asked, nor would it have the slightest bit of empathy or sympathy in its voice when it did. It showed no weakness in its persistence and demanded the truth from whom the question was asked, me.

With no college or trade school under my belt, my future seemed limited. I was scared and had no answers for this persistent repetitive question of, "What will I be when I grow up?"

My identity was slipping away as we disappeared farther from my hometown. I was naked. The Midwest will always be my bloodline, but the life I was living needed to bleed out. And so bleed out I did. Finally closing my eyes, I faded out down the road and into the unknown.

At times, this felt more like an ambulance ride than a bus ride. Everyone seemed to be nursing an injury in one way or another; even the driver seemed a bit shell-shocked and distant. The wounds of a hundred battles could be seen like invisible ghosts unwilling to pass into the realm of rest. It was always late into the night when the silent cries of the wounded awakened my slumbering soul.

When the last shot has been fired and triage has been started, the wounded lay helpless with pleading moans of mercy. Screams and whispers all sound the same, in true desperation for life again.

We were all heading to our chosen and or destined new lives/hospitals. Hopefully we would all make it in time, though some of us looked barely alive and as if heading for the morgue already.

Once again, it's late-night count, so I'll finish this up. As the guard passes by, I keep on writing with my back to the door, as if I don't hear him. I don't always get the flashlight in the eyes when I'm sitting here at my steel desk. By the time I turn around, he's usually gone to the next cell anyway. Unless he's rude and hits my door when looking in or I'm curious to see who's working the nightshift. I'll just sit and ignore them and keep on writing. Sometimes it feels pretty good to act as if they're not even there.

Try to imagine this right now as you're reading this: Someone can, is, or could at this very moment, take a peek into your window and look right at you and whatever you might be doing. Can you feel him? He's looking right now, or maybe he's not? But you think you've heard something just outside your window. Could you be on display twenty-four hours a day, never knowing if they're coming or if they're going?

Any sort of privacy in prison is an illusion. This prison cell is my house and my home. It's also my living room, my TV room, my bedroom, my bathroom, and even sometimes my kitchen and my dining room. Right now, later on, or in two minutes, they can come and look into any one of these worlds of mine, and there's not a thing I can do about it. There are no doors, windows, walls, shades, or curtains that keep them from seeing you.

Every now and then, everyone feels the need for some alone time. That's why I sometimes act like they're just not even there.

And I get to live like this why? Oh yeah, one night I *chose* to drive after drinking.

I might not be able to write tomorrow night because of my transfer. They (DOC) box and take all your things until you get settled into the new prison yard. I'm happy to be finally moving to another prison and a lower-security unit.

Oh, by the way, the second bus ride I talked a little bit about earlier. It was the bus ride here. The ride here to this prison was not at all like the long days of riding from Chicago but only a few hours at most, though it was still the longest ride I had ever taken in my life.

THIRTEEN

It's around 2:00 a.m., and I still can't fall asleep. It's my last night here in *this* Arizona State Penitentiary. I will leave here early this morning for a minimum security unit. So much has happened in the last year that it's really hard to wind down from it all. I'm a little scared at the moment, anticipating what's to come.

Sound a little familiar? Yep, it reads like the opening page of this book. Except I really don't have any fear like I did when coming here. It's more of a "position of readiness" that I have now.

As my eyes began to open on this newly light day, I knew something had gone missing, but I just couldn't say. I looked inside and out before I figured it out. They'd packed their bag in the cover of night and just slipped on out so we wouldn't fight. The note was clear, precise, and right to the point.

"I'm so sorry, but I can't live here anymore. I've seen way too much outside your prison door."

With love,
Innocence.

I too am now a seasoned man. Like the men I saw on my first day while walking across the prison yard.

How unpredictably predictable the prison world lives.

I've now finished my first tour within the prison world, and don't forget, there's no boot camp for convicts. I always made my workouts fairly tough on myself. Remember, "the battle is won on the training field." I've never been this fit emotionally, mentally, physically, and spiritually, at least never all at the same time. Precision tuned and ready for my second tour.

In the last year, I've seen some incredibly crazy things. Actually, it would only be crazy if I were still living in the free world. As for prison, it's the regular daily happenings around here and not that big of a deal. That's what makes it absolutely crazy. A day inside here is a walk in the park for us, but for the regular guys of the free world, this would be a walk in a minefield.

I'm not making light of prison, so don't get me wrong. It's quite the opposite. We have become so accustomed to the insanity within the lives we live that it's sanely normal.

For instance, a few months ago, Mike and I were on the weight pile. The sun was rather strong and sharp that day, as if we're in higher altitude. The perfect spring afternoon in the hot Arizona desert. Prison or not, it was a beautiful day outside. It was shortly after lunch ended, and Mike and I had the day off work. The yard was fairly quiet because most guys had already gone back to work for the afternoon, except for the few hiding out playing hooky. Besides Mike and myself, there were a couple others lifting and hanging out.

Some guys would be seen almost daily out on the phones after lunch. Even in the heat of the day, they'd stand there taking a sun lashing so they could talk to their loved ones or whoever it was. It was important no matter who, because some guys would literally stand there, talking for hours in the hot Arizona sun like it was nothing.

Phones can be hard to come by at night, depending on the day of the week. If you wrote a letter telling so and so that you'd call on such and such a night at such and such time and then someone is phone-hogging, so you can't make the call! Wars have been started for less. So if you had a person to call in the daytime, that would be the best time.

I know of this one so-called big guy that thought he could take a phone away from this long-winded littler guy, right in the middle of his call. Well, the little guy, mad as he could be, came back a few minutes later to take back his newly stolen phone. He marched straight over to that big guy as he was talking and laughing to whoever on the other end. He stuck the guy in the side of the neck with a sharp homemade prison shank. The big guy dropped the phone and ran off down the yard squealing like a stuck pig. And the little guy ran after him, trying to stick him some more. I heard they wound up at the weight pile fighting with a weight bar and shank in hand, when DOC finally reached them to break it up. Not sure what happed to them, but I never saw either one of them again.

Anyway, Mike and I were on the weigh pile, lifting, when we hear this guy yelling on the phone (at his wife, we found out later). It's not the first time anybody's heard a person yelling when on the prison yard phone. This is fairly common for some. But then, this guy became even more irate and started slamming the phone receiver on the block wall that the phone is mounted to, which is actually the control room's outside wall.

That's when we both looked over at him, about twenty five feet away, as he screamed into the phone, "Oh yeah, how do you like the sound of this!" We simultaneously heard this strange amplified choking sound coming from the man as we watched him slit his own throat. He dropped the receiver and fell to his knees with a dazed look. His face and torso followed shortly after, slamming into the dusty hard ground.

I asked Mike if he saw what I just saw. We both took a step closer toward the phones but stayed on the weight pile. Mike said, "Yeah, dude, he cut his own throat!" In which, I replied, "Dang, bro, that's crazy!" We stared for just a second before turning and walked back to our workout like it never happened. A few guards rushed out of their control room and tended to the fallen man. Someone cranked up the volume on their music box, and we all got back to the business of our workouts.

Three days later, I saw the slit-throat man back on the yard with a large bandage across his throat. I guess the cut didn't kill him. But to put him back on the yard after that? Now that's *insane*, but par for the course in prison.

The cruelty can come from both sides of the bars. Neither side would admit to this because their tactics would be different from each other's, but inmates and guards can be parallel in these matters.

When I first got here, there was a guy named Ted that lived in the pod next door. He was really a pretty big guy, like six feet six inches big. He had a pretty big mouth on him also and was always joking around with guys on the yard and drawing attention to himself. One day, as some of us were just hanging around outside our cells and talking, I asked Crunch if he'd seen Ted around.

Our tier seemed kind of quiet lately, so I was wondering what happed to him. Did he get rolled up and reclassified? Mike was standing there with us and chimed right on in. Mike always knows what the talk on the yard is. Ted had to PC up (protective custody) about a week or so ago. I was totally shocked, but Crunch seemed to already have known and all the details that proceeded.

It so happens that Ted was getting involved with the wrong guys on the yard, and then he tried acting like a lion when really Ted was just a lamb. Who knows what he did wrong or what was asked of him to do.

It's kind of like this. When you're asked to become a prospect for a certain club and you accept, you'll be asked to do certain things to show your loyalty and dedication, long before they would consider bringing you in as a full-fledged member. And if you don't measure up? Well, I don't know?

All I know is, these guys grabbed him one day and pulled him into a cell. I guess a bunch of them held him down as one of them tattooed some crazy things on Ted's chest.

The tattoo was pretty hard core . . . a picture of a man's genitals, with the word PUNK written underneath it all. I didn't think this to be anything less than a death sentence for him, no matter what the circumstances. Ted was told to PC up after that.

You'd think they would have taken care of this problem a little more quickly. It sounds like someone thought it best that he suffer a slow and humiliating sentence for his crimes against them.

I'm sure this whole ordeal will be like a nasty cancer eating upon his mind as he sits in PC for the rest of his time. I'm not sure how many more years he has inside prison, but literally, this has the power to end his life anytime outside the protection of protective custody and maybe even inside. We've all heard it said, "Once in PC, always in PC." We never did see Ted again after that.

There are quite a few tattoo artists in prison. A tattoo gun can be made from a striped motor of a tape player deck from a person's radio. Everyone knows this.

I believe the needle is made from a regular old paperclip or whatever else can be sharpened down to a point. It's the ink that's hard to come by, so a lot of guys make their own.

I watched a guy burn a small Styrofoam cup in his cell one day. He caught the black ash with another upside down cup as the smoke and ash floated above the flames.

Once the black ash was collected, he added a few small drops of shampoo and mixed it into a black ink substance. I was amazed with the ingenuity of this ink-producing process. I asked if he was afraid of getting an infection by using this kind of ink. He said, "No, that doesn't scare me. I'm more worried about getting caught with my tattoo gun and having to spend time in the hole."

You'd think that without matches or a lighter, there'd be no way of getting fire, right? Wrong. It's usually no problem at all. I've seen only parts of this process performed.

To start, you would need to take the lead out of one of your pencils. This is done by carefully splitting the pencil straight down the middle, with the now illegal razor that you have taken out of your legal disposable razor.

A piece of toilet paper is wrapped around the end of the lead and inserted inside the electric wall receptacle, which sparks onto toilet paper and lights the fire. It can sometimes blow the fuse to the power in your cell and other cells. DOC will write you up if they think you've been messing with the receptacle. Most of the time, this is performed only as a last resort.

Inside most of the cells, you can see where this has been done. If you just look above the receptacle on the wall, you can see a black burn mark on the paint where the flame has licked it.

It's really pretty cool to see the ideas inmates have come up with to solve different problems. Like making a "fire donut" so you can heat something up without all the smoke and fire.

To make a donut, you'd first take a roll of TP and start wrapping it around your hand until you have gotten a good strong paper ring around your hand. Then hold the ring in both hands and start turning the inside of the ring through to the outside of itself. This will twist the TP in a tight ring. When you light the donut, you light the inside of the ring, not the outside. Now you have a slow-burning fire without all the smoke. You burn the donut on your toilet rim, so you can flush the smoke down when needed and when the fire needs to disappear.

Some guys will heat up coffee doing this, and some guys will cook something using this. I've done this only once, and that was to warm myself on the coldest night of my life.

For some reason, the heat was not blowing into my vent on this unseasonably cold winter night. You wouldn't think that the Arizona desert would ever be anything but hot, but I'm telling you, I've never been so cold in all my life. Remember I grew up in Chicago so I'm no stranger to seeing my breath. It must have been the block walls of my cell that held in the cold the way it did.

I would've felt warmer hanging on a meat-hook inside some slaughterhouse meat locker. I banged on my cell door and yelled through the window in protest just as most of the others did in my pod.

As we continued hounding DOC about the heating issue, they continued with all their typical answers: "We're working on it," "Okay, I'll see what I can do," and "Let me check with the sergeant, and I'll get back to you." It's always the same old answer with them. They know they can get away with just about any answer when you're behind the glass of a prison cell door.

This isn't the first time this has happened, though before it was about the cooling. It must have been 100 degrees the time we were locked down on a code red, and it was so hot you couldn't breathe. I put water on myself and lay down on my cell floor to stay cool that day.

You start learning the DOC modem of operation early on in prison. They like it best when we're all locked down in our cells. This way, they can do whatever they want and not have to worry about watching us inmates. We can see them as they sit hiding in their control room, waiting for their shift to end.

While leaving us frustrated, angry, and without, they head home to the comforts and concerns of their free life. And as the night shift arrives with torches in hand, they too surrender no answers concerning our heating situation. This is the norm for the life we live in prison.

To keep from getting hypothermia or freezing to death, I put on almost every piece of clothing I had.

As crazy as it sounds, I put on two pair of blue jeans and a pair of sweatpants over them. I could only put on two pair of socks because my boots couldn't fit on my feet with three. I also had on three T-shirts, two button-down shirts, a sweatshirt, and my winter-lined prison-issued denim jacket. To complete my fashion ensemble, I had on my prison beanie hat pulled down over my ears and half my eyes. What a look that must have been.

I moved like a tin man who couldn't find his oil can. I only needed to get into bed and under my covers, though that was no more than a bed sheet and a thin wool blanket. I was really hoping that the breath from my lungs would warm me up under the covers, at least long enough so I could stop shivering.

I eventually fell asleep, but I kept waking up through the night with no warmth in sight. So I just held on tight and froze in my bed all night.

Once again, all I could think about was, "All this because I chose to drive after drinking?" Yes, yes, yes! It's crazy how that thought relentlessly keeps coming.

FOURTEEN

Late one December night, the doom of darkness danced with delight.

For he knew I had no might for the fight in the absence of the light.

When he found me sleeping and delinquent at my post, he realized I'd be helpless and just give up the ghost.

The thief came sneaking silently out of sight and swiftly commenced to destroy my life.

Protecting the dream. It was not so long ago that I too held on to my very own dream—becoming a U.S. Marine. Now it lies hostage, locked away by the chains of my own making, along with all the other precious gems that a free life holds. Felons cannot become Marines. Unfortunately, I didn't understand the importance or value of protecting the dream.

Are you protecting the dream? Will you take this as seriously as the thief does? Will he find you standing guard at the duty of your post, or just sleeping in the cover of darkness like most?

Like most people, I never did look at my life in this manner before I came to prison, but now I'm fully aware of the consequences for not doing so. You see, there are billions upon billions of dreams, out there just waiting to be fulfilled. There's also dream destroyers out there. They lay in waiting around every corner, determined to destroy the dream.

It had taken me quite some time to even realize I had a dream. In high school, I had no idea what I might want to be or do in life. I looked and looked, but nothing ever lit my fuse. It's pretty hard seeing other people dreaming the big dream and knowing exactly what they want to be, and you yourself not having even a clue. No one ever told me that my dream would eventually dawn on me and to just hold on until it did. But that's what I did.

My older brother David is one of those people that I watched protecting the dream. He had already known when we were small child that he wanted to fly airplanes out of O'Hare airport in Chicago, and that's exactly what he's doing today. I thought I would never find a dream like that, though I still secretly hoped I would.

I didn't know this before now, but I'm sure that my parents were looking at me in this way. I was the dream, their dream, and they were protecting it at all cost. As parents, they knew that someday I'd realize I had a dream inside me. And if my parents were not around, then it was somebody like a teacher or a coach or even a cop here and there. They were all showing me in one way or another that I too would find a dream to live for.

What did all of them have in common? They were looking out for me and my dream, directly or indirectly. But how was I to know there would be such a dream. I thought, they were trying to run my life, and they didn't have a clue about what I needed or wanted. I wish I'd realized back then that grown-ups are just old kids.

I had no idea that a dream would ever come to the surface of myself. Where does this passion, this spark of life come from? It seems as if suddenly, it came out of nowhere one day, burning throughout my bones like a wildfire and consuming all that even slightly threatened its destiny. In an instant, it breathes the breath of life.

The dream sometimes lays hidden deep within, or it can be out in the open shining out loud for all to adore. But a dream is not a dream until its breath arrives, until then, it is nothing more than a fleeting thought.

Dreams and thoughts differ in one way only . . .

Thoughts are perceived pictures within one's mind and possess no lasting life. Dreams are perceived pictures within one's spirit that breathes passion and life into action.

Dreams are born deep within your soul. As your spirit reaches to receive your newborn dream wrapped in all its warmth and tenderness, the awe of its origination will overflow within you before spilling out for all the world to see.

The tears of lost dreams seem to fall forever, cleansing and clearing the path for the next generation of dreams to come. For life is but a dream . . .

Today I'm living within this prison; today from within this prison, I hold a dream. I have actually held this dream my whole life, though until recently I didn't know it was a dream. Then I felt its breath within me.

A family man. I dream of being a husband and a dad. That's my dream; that's always been my dream. Having a wife and some kids running around would be a dream come true for myself. I thought being a Marine was my only dream until I looked a little deeper and realized I had a few other dreams alongside. So how do I know what my true dreams are? I know what they are when I look inside and see my true self, that person I am aching to be, the real me.

So how does a felon or an ex-felon ever become a husband and dad? How do I get to the white picket fence? What road do I take to get there? How long is the walk? Where do I even begin this journey of the family man, and how will I ever support them? The dream is well and alive, but the road is unknown at present.

I trust that someday it will be clear to me as I look back as an old man smiling. For now, I will seek daily guidance as I journey on this new road of life.

Trusting that whatever has been put inside me to be and to do, I will achieve with all grace love and guidance. We must only seek and move forward. It is in the journey, not the destination, that we find our true selves and the dreams that follow.

Dang! There goes the bright flashlight in the eyes again. I turned right into it as the guard was walking by and looking in doing the late count. They must really stress these guys at training school to shine that bright-ass light into our eyes even when our cell light is on. Why? The only reason I can come up with is they want to show power over us by reaching in with that light and touching us with it.

Everything that takes my eyes off my dream is the enemy . . . guards, inmates, bad phone calls, fears, worries, stresses, whoever, whatever.

All sorts of things can take our eyes away from our purpose. I pretty much know the why and what of my life here on earth, but I sometimes get pulled into the illusions of this world, though they are counterfeit and hold no real life.

I'm not a very happy person when I close the sunroof of my life and allow the liar to hold me close and tight. I'm not sure why I allow this to occur with all the glorious wonders that surround me, but I sometimes still do.

I believe that certain people can sense the wonderful dream that another carries, and they will do almost anything to destroy that which they do not possess. I'm not sure why, but I know this to be true. It could be that the essence of life shines so bright through the faith of a person's dream, that the destroyer becomes blinded with murderous rage.

How incredible it is when your dream is first born! You really start beginning to know who, what, and where you are. Oh, how wonderful the day the dream is born!

The dream is like the great lion. It knows what it is from the very start and desires to be nothing else. The dream and the lion live as one.

FIFTEEN

Not long before prison, I meet an old woman. I was at the hospital sitting by the window and waiting on my brother. He was having some test done, and I went to check on him. As I sat waiting and looking out that big picture window, I'd notice this woman from time to time coming closer from just down the hall. She was moving painfully slow.

What was so important to this old woman that she'd walk the obstacles of a fifty-yard hallway. She and the IV stand were as one. It led her every step of the way. It was just short of eternity when she made her way to where I sat. With a sad smile, she stood squinting, gazing upon the landscape five stories below.

The sun was bright that morning as we both stared out into the day. I instinctively understood her plot as she stood their staring. So many dreams still lived inside her, but they'd been incarcerated by fear. Her head now bowed and eyes closed. She cried quietly as tears flowed from her soul. She whispered softly, "My god, if for only one more day."

I wonder how many people actually go out of this world thinking they've missed out on becoming who they're supposed to be. That scares me. If there's one thing I should be afraid of, then it should be of not becoming what I was created to be.

Every human on this planet has in their mind's eye the person they desire to be. Where does that image come from? Is it of our own making? Or God-given?

It's in our DNA from the beginning for sure. Like rows of seed in a field, it waits to sprout. Just add water. We all have that picture in our mind's eye of the person and life we want to become. Faith is the water that spouts the seed. Don't ever let someone tell you (not even yourself) that you can't be who you were made to be.

The lion knows who he is, the lion. He also knows what he is, the king of the jungle.

It's pretty late, the guard let me have this pencil and paper so I could at least write tonight. All my things have been boxed up and are gone. Technically they could transfer me at any time.

This cell is bare and empty tonight. No TV, no radio, no books, no potted plant, no photos of family and friends, no bath mat at the foot of my bed covering the cold concrete floor. Nothing.

My cell was decked out and very prison livable. Still a prison cell, but I made it nicer than most.

After a year in this cell, I accumulated quite a few things and made it as much like any home as possible. You'd think all prison cells were created equal, but that's far from fact. My cell was a true man cave. Safe. Secure. Solitude.

It feels pretty raw tonight, like when I first arrived here. I'm on guard and very alert. I'll soon be leaving and venturing into the unknown. The enemy will be everywhere.

It's the calm before the storm. Adrenaline rushes through my veins like a flashflood. Through I remain peaceful and steady, I'm bridling the strength of a one hundred stallions.

At any time they will hit the switch from the control room, and I will hear my door unlock for the last time. The yard is lit up bright, just as it has been every night that I've been here. Except tonight, I will go through the curtain of darkness and into the night on the other side.

I have been here at Santa Cruz prison for approximately one year. I've spent each night from 9:00 p.m. to 7:00 a.m. locked inside this prison cell. That's not including daytime counts and code red lockdowns.

Each night I've gazed into the unknown black hole just beyond the fence line. How will it feel to be inside the other side once again?

Home . . . the place they know you as you.

SIXTEEN

Click, click. The guard in control just hit my door switch a couple of times. They do that sometimes to get your attention.

He must have thought I was asleep. There is still a mattress in here, but who could sleep waiting to be transferred.

I reach for the door, holding my breath. Silence surrounds me. Suddenly, I feel the cool night air fill my lungs. Exhaling with ecstasy, I can taste freedom on my lips.

Before I even looked up, I sensed the stars staring down upon me. They were amazed to see me, as I them. I sparkled with delight, watching them twinkle throughout the night.

This is like a dream. I closed my cell door one last time. At the end of the tier, I glance into Eddy's old cell. It's been empty a couple of months, and I miss him. I remember some of the talks we had just before lockdowns.

It seems I have the planet to myself. My god, this is overwhelming . . .

Then, I see another inmate coming from the next pod over. I guess there's two of us transferring out tonight. Not sure if I know him or if I've seen him before.

A guard meets us about halfway from the control room, and we start the long walk across the prison yard. We're on our way to the administration building and main transport area.

As we go through the sally port and into the transport building, the guard drops us off to another officer who informs us both that it might be a while before we load up on the bus and leave.

We are both put into a small transport holding cell by the second officer as the first officer slips out of sight and back to his nightshift duties. The clock is always running in here for us, so what does it really matter where we do our time. That's the look we both gave each other as we sit down on the hard wooden benches.

He and I both know we're not cut from the same cloth, so we ended up saying absolutely nothing to one another as we sat and waited. Prison is all about waiting for something to happen or for something not to happen, but you better be ready for both.

It won't be long, no matter how long we have to sit in here and wait. Soon we'll be on that prison bus heading down the road somewhere and looking out the window into the free world. I'll finally get to see it again after all this time. How cool is that! This is going to be better than just about anything I've done all year. I'm actually going to get a glimpse into the free world today, though it will be through bars, but who cares. The window could be as little as a tiny peep hole for all I care; I'm going to see the world again today.

It's about 7:00 a.m., and they've got us moving on the road. The prison bus is actually a fifteen-passenger van with blacked-out windows. We can see out, but the world can't see in. We are going north somewhere, but they won't tell us any destinations. It's all about security.

We are heavily locked and caged within this van. We have also been chained together with ankle and waist chains. To top it all off, we're handcuffed to our own waist chains. Try and scratch an itch. Good luck with that.

There are twelve inmates in this bus, along with one driving and one shotgun guard who is armed and ready behind a thick cage.

There are a few high-risk inmates on this bus, and they must be going to maximum or the like. Maybe to Florence or even Tucson's supper max. Even a guy like myself that's going to a minimum security unit has to endure the high-security ride.

Florence, I believe, is the oldest prison in Arizona and has what's called Central Unit or The Walls. It's a maximum security unit with a few more hardcore units alongside.

Tucson has been called Gladiator school. There are a few different units down there also, including CDU, which stands for Central Detention Unit or otherwise known as Super Max. It's also called the hole. You can be in the hole at any prison unit. The hole means you're locked down without your stuff for 24-7. It's the end of the line. It doesn't get any tighter than Super Maximum in the prison world.

The way we are all chained together, I think they're heading down south for some hard time.

That inmate that came with me from Santa Cruz is a hard one for sure. After a little time in prison, you can tell who's really a hard guy and who's not. I can see the hate in his eyes as he looks at other inmates. We both understand the golden rule. He lives on one side of the fence, and I live on the other. I don't pee on his lawn, and he doesn't pee on mine. Like a tolerable neighbor, we say hello in passing. Anything more, or less, could be war.

It's so weird to feel the vehicle moving beneath me and to see the sights outside my window change. The lighting out here even looks unfamiliar as it's lying across the landscape. All my senses are overloaded as they try to recalibrate and adjust to the lights, colors, sounds, smells, and speeds. Having to focus and then refocus at the incredibly fast-moving cars is enough by itself to spin my head.

It's kind of like waking up from a long sleep and then stepping directly into the big top tent of a circus. Without acclimating to your new environment, you're a little overwhelmed.

It's around 8:00 a.m. on Monday morning, and things haven't changed that much when it comes to traffic. People are running late for work with one eye closed and the pedal to the metal.

On the flip side, it's so very peaceful out here on the road and the other side of the fence. The colors I'm seeing are just crazy on my brain, like fireworks on the Fourth. I've never in my life seen such brilliant colors. I had no idea how weak my sight was. You just can't see until you can see.

That makes me wonder about all these people driving to their jobs today. Do they know where they are going? Are they going to where they want to go? Myself, I have no choice at the moment.

We all have to make a living. But why do some of us settle in life and not keep moving forward into the life that calls to us?

I'm the guy in prison. I'm the guy talking from the grave. I'm not there to live my calling. I'm chained up. What a waste of life not being who you are. I've been disqualified, and I'm waiting for the next race. Run the good race.

Even with chains on my hands and feet, I'm planning and working toward my new life. When the prison gate finally opens and sets me free, I'll be wasting no time sprinting into the life that waits for me. The dream waits.

Without a coach to train me, I'm not sure I'd have a chance in the race. Craig has been a great life coach and friend. May I suggest that you find one. When you are truly ready, he will appear.

When they put up a high-rise building, they dig deep into the ground and secure a solid foundation. Without, the skyscraper would never stand the test of time.

If my life is going to scrape the sky, my foundation cannot be that of a house. Build as high or as low as you would like. But build so it will not fail inside the storms of life.

I have just finished my first year in prison. It was the hardest year of my life. Because of *one* bad choice, *one* bad night. My life has been crushed into little, tiny pebbles and sent back into the Stone Age. No Marine Corps, no girlfriend, no job, no family and friends. And ironically, I have no freedom inside the world's freest country.

Those are just a few of the things that I have lost; it would take more than the pages of this book to list them all. But to be fair, the choices of that night cost others much more than it cost myself.

The victims, the courts, the authorities, my attorneys. They never even let me know how these guy's weathered that horrific night. Big price tag for a night of partying. Don't forget the families and friends that suffered through this whole thing.

We've stopped at four prisons today. The prisons look much the same on the outside; it's what's on the inside that scares people. You get to hear stories about each one of them from different guys along the way. Some stories are funny, some sickening, and others should be unrepeatable.

We've spent over nine hours riding on this bus, and there are only three inmates left. If only these guys could stop talking for a few minutes, I've heard quite enough convict stories for one day.

Being that we're all transferring to the same minimum security unit, they finally took off our handcuffs and chains at the last prison we stopped at. We started off going north today, and then we turned south and now we're going north again. The sun is slowly starting to set, and it's absolutely breathtaking. I'm one step closer to the gate with this prison transfer, and I look forward to the freedoms that now come with my minimum security classification.

It's well after 5:00 p.m., and we just arrived at the minimum security prison. It feels strange in here. It only has a nine foot fence and with no razor wire—no razor wire! We drove right inside the open prison gates, and no one even closed them behind us. A guard sits at the gate in a guard shack, but the gate stays open until night-time count. It has more of the feel of a summer boys' camp than that of a prison.

They let the three of us into the chow hall to eat, and we were all freaking out a bit because of the plates and silverware we were now using. Real silverware and real plates. At the high- and medium-security prisons, we used plastic trays and plastic sporks. That's a spoon and a fork as one. Here at minimum, you could take a real knife into your hand. As an inmate that's done some time, you can't help but think about the power you now hold as you're holding a real knife or fork in your hand once again.

Dinner for general population was already over, so we were in the chow hall all by ourselves. The food was much better and a definite treat, and you could eat all that you wanted to. They also have this big cold milk dispenser. You could drink all the milk you wanted. Is that ever great. Pretty nice setup in their kitchen, that's for sure, and we agreed we could all get fat here at this unit. We all walked out of there bursting full and very satisfied.

It was now time to find our assigned bunks. This unit has Quonset huts for housing. There are about twenty-five prisoners per Quonset hut. We all stopped at the control room and picked up our box of belongings before heading off to our new house. I'm not sure how many inmates are in this unit, but from its size, it looks to be about four hundred or so.

It might really be strange not sleeping in a prison cell tonight and being out in the open. Out in the wide open, sleeping in a hut with a bunch of other inmates. This doesn't sound real safe to me, and I'm not so sure I like it.

When you first walk into this Quonset, you can see its uniform bunks all the way down to the door at the end. There is absolutely no privacy whatsoever. When you look either left or right, they're exactly the same.

There are these old rusty metal bunks with beat-up dingy mattress on them. They all run along the wall with an eight-foot-high wooden locker at the outside and head of each bed. There is also a horizontal cabinet attached to the top of the locker which runs across the head of the bed and attaches to the wall.

Between the vertical locker and the horizontal cabinet there is a piece of eight by four wood panel. This works as a kind of headboard between you and the next guy. Though there is separation between headboards and bunks on the same side of the hut, there is nothing separating us from the guys on the mirrored side of us.

When you walk in the front door and all the way down to the bathroom and showers, you walk right down the middle of the hut and past every guy that might be siting or sleeping on his bunk. That's what I call absolutely no privacy. And after living in a cell for little over a year, I'm not sure I can do this here. Will see.

The bathrooms are pretty big and have mirrors on the walls. It's weird to see yourself in a big mirror after only seeing your face in a four-inch mirror for the last year. I'm a lot bigger than I thought I was. The toilets sit in a row down the wall, with real toilets seats. The shower room has about fifteen shower heads. I'm not real big on the group showering, and it's only because I know some guys are.

I'm not sure how well I'll settle into this place. It's the fact that I don't have a cell to put my back up against. Maybe this last year has changed me more than I thought it did.

This place is a war zone without the front line, and the enemy wears the same uniform.

SEVENTEEN

I've been at this minimum-security unit for several months now, and I just can't take it one more minute.

It sure didn't start out that way. I kind of thought I'd like it here at first, but then, not long after, the place showed it's true colors.

The warden, guards, and staff treat the inmates like bribed children, and we in return act as bribed children do.

What's the bribe? The bribe is all the secret amenities of this minimum unit, and they are plentiful.

What do they get for the bribe? They get all the skills and labor they desire, for just about nothing. And "they" means the townspeople.

Most inmates go into town daily. Everything from trash collectors, landscapers, welders, heavy equipment operators, carpenters, you name it. There are many more trades and services represented in their pool of prison workers. "Just about nothing" means approximately twenty-five cents an hour.

Sounds really good if you're the townspeople. Lower taxes and jobs are getting done for practically nothing. And don't forget you're doing a good service for mankind by putting the poor inmate back to work and getting him ready to be a part of society once again. Right? Ha ha, sure you are.

Unfortunately, that's what it looks like from the outside, but that's not what's really going on from the inside. As like most dysfunctional families, it can all look wonderful on the outside, but the inside needs some real work.

Every morning, four of the prison buses load up with inmates and head for town. They are followed by a guard in a pickup truck. I think this is because all the buses are driven by inmates and until the bus stops at their designated sites they could be used as getaway cars, so to speak.

Here's a little peek into a few of our amenities, and why we behave as if we're bribed children.

Not a day goes by that either drugs or alcohol does not enter the prison. Anything can be dropped in town for an inmate to pick up. Some local woman find inmates to be quite attractive. "Secret amenity."

Inmates in town are not supervised for most of their working hours. Though there is a guard whose job it is to drive around from site to site checking on the inmates at their worksites.

There is a reason that most inmates don't take advantage of the prison chow hall. I guess when you're eating homemade food all day, why would you bother eating prison food. "Secret amenity."

Cindy came here to see me when I first arrived, but it's so far from Phoenix that the visitation time was even shorter than the time it took for her to drive here. Funny though, just the other day, this guy said his girlfriend came to see him and they had a few good hours together. But wait, that was on a Wednesday, and visitation is on Saturday and Sunday. "Secret amenity."

Lots of new tattoos at this unit. I hear ink and tat guns are pretty easy to come by. "Secret amenity."

There are many more secret amenities. I mentioned the ones that are common knowledge to both sides of the fence.

I myself won't walk around here with the face of a bribed child, not for a few sodas and ice cream.

That's all they really have to get me with, soda and ice cream. I don't play on the other side of the tracks anymore, so they don't have any of the other stuff to entice me with.

I hadn't had soda or ice cream for a long time before I came here to this unit. They have an inmate store with just about anything you'd like to buy. It was a bit of a treat at first, but now it's just soda and ice cream. They have no carrot on a stick, no bribe for me to stay here.

I have less here at this unit than what I had at my last unit. Visits are not going to happen for me, because of the distance we are from Phoenix. And I miss having my own prison cell.

What really gets me about this place is the "no walking on the grass" rule. They have this huge beautiful green lawn in which all the buildings sit around. I'm extremely irritated with the "no walking on the grass" enforcement.

If soda and ice cream aren't my thing, what are the amenities that keep me here? The prison knows what keeps the inmates working, and the inmates know what keeps the prison working.

Though on the map we are pretty far north, the moral compass seems to have gone south.

Some inmates have never had it so good. I myself can't hardly stand this place. Here's a few more reasons why.

First, this place reeks horribly of hypocrisy. The noise inside here is constant. When I had a prison cell, I could always turn my radio on and drown out the unwanted sounds.

At lights out, you are not allowed to have your TV or radio playing, even with your headphones. Are you kidding! Am I three years old and need to be told what time I should go to sleep.

One night, this hunched-over old man came slowly shuffling through our house. I thought maybe at first he was lost from some retirement home, but then realized he was a guard doing late-night count. He shined his flashlight straight into my face and eyes. Yes, even here I still get the bright flashlight in the eyes.

It was obvious he was unhappy just by the way he sneered over the rims of his glasses, mean and squinty eyed. Snapping at me for not quickly responding to his grumpy request of "lights and music off." Wisely, he kept his turtle-like pace moving down the row before some young rabbit snatched him up and shook him like a rag doll.

Sometimes it's almost too much to hold back, like the caged power of an angry gorilla. He nor I can truly gauge the strength that beholds the great silverback.

Try sleeping in a large room with twenty-five other guys. It's nothing short of insomnia. Imagine the snoring, sniffling, and coughing that's going on under one roof. Besides that, there's the night screams of the haunted. Waking late at night from their torturous nightmares, they find themselves living within another. The nights are restless.

It really feels unsafe living out in the open. I really miss my prison cell. Besides having my own cave to slip away to, it was a place of safety and calmness. I think most guys would agree that their prison cells were like an embassy within a foreign land.

I already know of one guy since I've been here that had his brains bashed in as he slept on his bunk. All I know is someone took a steel pipe and caved this guy's head in as he slept. They say he will live, but he'll never be the same again. Don't be silly; of course no one knows who did it, and I'm sure no one ever will.

Some guy was stabbed three times the other day. Sounds like someone really wanted him dead. But he lived. That same week, a guy was shanked in the thigh and almost bleed out before DOC got to him. Later, it was said he actually shanked himself, so he could get off of this yard. Remember this is a minimum unit.

Sometimes an inmate will owe a debt he just can't pay. He will do anything to get off the yard before the debt collectors get to him. Usually the borrower will do something that can't necessarily be detected as true or false by the debt collectors themselves. Like if a guy is stabbed and has to go to the hospital, his debt would still be delinquent but not by his default. He would most likely be granted a little grace on the timeline of this debt, if this be true.

Some inmates that are trying to avoid their debts will get a few write-ups so that they will go to the hole and then be unable to make payment. The lender and his collectors are usually wise to the games that are played out by their clients and act accordingly.

There's not much "emotionally mumbling" going on inside of prison. Meaning, nobody is looking at their shoes and skirting around the truth about how they really feel.

One weekend, I showed my true colors. It was a Saturday morning and well before noon. I was hoping to catch up on some overdue sleep. I thought most guys were thinking the same after a long hard week of work. I kept pulling my pillow over my head, hoping it would all quiet down after a while. They just kept getting louder and louder with their laughing and carrying on, playing cards like it was late afternoon.

Some dumb monkey thought that he could just walk on by and throw some old broken broom handle right into the big metal trashcan that sits just across from my bed area. To say that it echoed throughout the hut and rattled my brains would be an understatement.

Before I even knew what I was doing, I found myself up and out of bed, holding that broom handle. No "emotionally mumbling" here. Like only a silverback could, I broke that broom handle effortlessly into a million tiny splinters, along with a rampaging roar specifically warning the next person that makes noise. Putting myself on the endangered species list was not a smart idea, although at the moment, no one dared putting me in their sights for a takedown.

Back on my bunk, I stared at the ceiling waiting for the flush of adrenaline to finish its course. Wow, I can't believe I let that out of the cage. I'm really starting to get wound tight here at this unlivable unit.

It wasn't but about a week or two ago that I almost "tuned up" this guy they call Cowboy. I had just received a letter from Cindy and was intensely caught up reading it as I walked slowly through the narrow mail room hallway. She has not been writing to me as much as she used to, and I was in fear this could be the "Dear John" letter I had anticipated. It was not.

As I'm walking and reading with my head down, I felt this guy bump into me without saying a word. At first I didn't realize what had happened. Lifting my head, I saw him turn the corner and pass through the door. Suddenly I was enraged. How dare he bump me and keep walking. I quickly walked to the door, but he was gone. The more I thought about it, the more unreasonable I became. I wanted to rip his head off his body.

I searched throughout the unit with vengeance leading the way, but to no avail. I started asking others where I could find this guy, as I beat the brush from house to house. Somebody must know where this guy lives. Maybe they thought it best they mind their own business, especially after seeing the look of blood in my eyes.

I wanted this guy's head for what he did, though I knew mentally this reasoning was not the best move for me. Emotionally, the way of war seemed to make complete sense for the level of disrespect that was shown.

Suddenly, there he was as I rounded the corner. He was lying on his bunk reading a book, clueless that he was being hunted by a mad man. I stood over him at the foot of his bed, leaving him with plenty of room for which to stand. When he saw my eyes, he did a double take and knew exactly why I was there.

"What's up, Holmes?" was whispered with a nod and a cocky tone, as if he still had the power to save himself. Really.

"You jammed me in the hallway and kept walking." The sternness of my demeanor destroyed all his defenses. He was now sitting up against his pillow and searching frantically for the way around this or the courage to go through what he'd started.

He choose the way around. I heard his voice raise much louder now, so others would hopefully come and back him up. "You're crazy, dude. I don't know what you're talking about," was his shaky answer to the truth.

I spoke plain and simple, "Look, Holmes, you know you jammed me, so if you think you're all that, then stand your ass up."

His comeback was even louder now as he shouted in pure desperation. "You're crazy man! You're crazy!"

His voice carried throughout the Quonset hut like a trapped animal squealing in a snare. With the good speed of a mother hen, some busybody came from around the showers to see what little babe had been caught. He tried flapping his wings and puffing his chest out to chase me off. I told the muscle head sternly it would be best for him to mind his own business and get back to the showers. He too was smart enough to not square up with me in the moment and walked out, mumbling back to his shower.

I looked Cowboy straight in the eyes and told him he better stay clear of me. I turned and walked outside and into the sunshine of the day. Being that he never got off of his bunk throughout this whole ordeal told me all that I really needed to know.

I still hold on to the same morals today. No hurting someone unless I'm about it be. Then and only then, I'm in the clear to put the pain on someone. Cowboy was in the wrong for jamming me in the hallway; he and I both knew it. He also knew most guys would of tuned him up for that.

Lately it's been hard to be at peace, like I'm underwater, drowning. His voice is not getting through the deep and murky water. I feel alone floating here by myself. I'm going under, and no one seems to see me at this depth. Where's the lifeline? Won't anyone jump in? I can't hold my breath much longer.

I used to spend time with Him back in my cell late through the night. But now I don't have a place of solitude to commune with Him. God, what do I do.

I've been feeling insecure lately. Maybe it's because I'm getting closer to the streets. I'm clueless on what to do with my life the next time I'm in the free world. I'm scared that I'll be a failure again, even with a second chance and knowing where I went wrong. God, show me the map of my way and the road that you have laid before me.

EIGHTEEN

Well, I'm still hanging on here at this minimum unit. I realized that I'm really only at peace when I'm looking through the sunroof. When I close the sunroof of life, it sure gets dark fast.

I started talking to Him again within my mind and when I can (without looking crazy) out loud. Like when I'm out here in the sun raking rocks and working. I'm by myself at the fence line during the day and feel just fine speaking out loud as I move about. I'm also back to my daily running, my moving meditation.

For whatever reason, I got caught up in the daily life of this minimum unit. I started to tailspin downward after only a few months. This place is part prison and part streets, and that's what really messes with my head. It's like ice cream and cake one minute and chain you to the basement floor the next. I don't know how else to say it, but this place is darkness disguised as light.

I still don't like being here one bit more than before. But I just keep holding on until my time of freedom comes. I still have at least one more year until I can maybe parole out.

Here's a good example of darkness disguised as light:

I have been afflicted a few times in my past with pleurisy. This is a very painful lung infirmity where the lining of the lung gets stuck. I'm really not all that sure of what happens. But with every breath, agony comes calling.

It's so painful; the first time I thought it to be a heart attack and death on my doorstep. It happens mostly when I take a long hot shower and then come out into the cool night air. It had never happened in prison until now. I knew immediately what it was.

I got to see the doctor two days later—yes, two freaking days later! They really couldn't care less about your pain level as long as you're still moving.

I was going to fake a heart attack when I was working, so they would get me to the doctor. I still don't know why I didn't just fall down and wait for someone to come take me to the hospital.

The few times I have seen a doctor about pleurisy, they have always treated it with antibiotics and an inhaler. The physician I was finally able to see was a quack with honors.

Besides being in desperate need of retirement, this guy smelled like booze and slurred his words. Great, a drunken skeleton. Now I've seen it all.

He kept pushing on the left side of my chest saying, "It's a pulled muscle."

What he did next made me feel like I was in some crazy communist prison camp for scientific experiments.

The needle he was hovering over me with was the largest I'd ever seen. With a trembling hand, he told me to lay still.

He thought he was going to put that needle into my chest, just above my heart, and shoot me full of cortisone.

Now looking like mad-scientist from an old black-and-white movie, he smiled a little sideways.

I couldn't get off that cold medical table fast enough. I grabbed my T-shirt in one hand and the doorknob in the other. I said he was crazy and needed to study medicine as I slammed the door.

I was quickly meet by DOC out the front door and on the sidewalk. Three guards came down the sidewalk with the speed of linebackers, ready to rustle me to the ground. With my hands held high, I told them I was not out of control.

The doctor had called a 10-16 on his radio as I walked out. "10-16" is an out-of-control inmate. The guards stopped just short of tackling me and circled me instead. When I told them where I had been, they chuckled and let me go. This place could make even an angel a tad off his rocker.

Earlier I mentioned something about Cindy's letter. She seems to think I've changed and that my heart has become hard and cynical.

Well, where the ham sandwich does she think I'm at. The last time I looked, I was in prison. Some days are just better than others.

I've seen inmates participate with enthusiasm as they engage in endeavors of cruelty. They take and manipulate. They conquer whatever they can. They deceive others on a daily basis.

Maybe from the outside it looks like I've joined the hardhearted. But it's quite the contrary. I have put on the full armor and wear it well.

Prison is warfare, period! Most people believe prison is just a physical challenge. Living inside prison is emotionally, mentally, physically, and spiritually challenging. When I put on the armor, I'm balanced. But I don't always walk the line, as well as I'd like.

It's like the balancing weights of a car tire. If just one of them is missing, the whole tire spins off balance and wobbles. I am an emotional, mental, physical, and spiritual human being. Each part requires daily attention to stay safely balanced.

I can see Cindy's side of things. She's thinking my heart has become tainted. That's what hurts.

I really miss her. It's been months since she's kissed me with sunshine and whispered smiles into my heart. It's frustrating living apart. At Santa Cruz, I'd visit with her almost weekly. Visits keep a man's heart soft and pliable. Maybe that's why she hears a hardened tone when we talk on the phone.

We need not speak for open ears to hear, nor for closed eyes to see, but for broken hearts to beat.

My hope is that she understands. My hardened heart is just for a time. And it's still me behind the steel door. Though I put on the full armor of God and walk as a man, I sometimes feel more familiar fighting in my old war clothes. I'm fully confident, sooner or later, I will walk content within these new ones.

It's like a new pair of shoes that look and feel great in the store. You can hardly wait to wear them the first day. But they become a little hard to walk in, and you get a blister. You concede that they will need to be broken in slowly. With patience, the day finally comes, and those stiff and stubborn shoes are now the most comfortable ones you own.

Dang! I just got the bright light in the eyes. The night guard walked by doing count. I'm sitting on the end of my bed with me feet up. The overhead lights on, and he still shined the flashlight into my face as I'm sitting here writing.

As I was saying before, I think about Cindy a lot. Is she really going to be there for me when I'm out? I'm crazy about this girl, and I know she's crazy about me. With that said, I'm still feeling her slowly slipping away. Maybe she's waking up to the fact that I'm in prison. I'm now a convict, and when I'm out of here, I'll be an ex-convict.

We both know she could do a lot better. I think I'm starting to pull away from her too, as she's slowly pulling away from me. Her letters don't sound the same anymore. Something's missing from them.

I think my time has come for leaving this piece of hell behind. I hate this so-called prison. If I'm going to be locked up, it should be in a real prison, in a cell. I've got nothing to lose with my friends so far anyway.

What's it matter, I actually liked the higher-security prison. I've already learned that people are crazy at every unit level. There are more bad guys per capita in this unit than a lot of other units.

You can just feel DOC laughing behind your back for being at the bottom of life. They act as if it's a privilege for us to go out and do their dirty work for them.

Like I said, they've got nothing for me in the trade. Everyone is dying to be here at this wonderful unit. No one would do anything to jeopardize themselves from being taken away. I've heard inmates talking about this place like it's the promised land or something.

Myself, it's best I leave before I do something I really regret. I've seen too many inmates get more time, as they're doing time. I don't want that. I'm out of here.

NINETEEN

It's 9:00 p.m. on Sunday, and I just rolled up. Are they ever mad. I threw all my things in a box and walked up to the control room and knocked on the glass window. The guard asked, "What can I do for you?"

"You can get me off this yard."

When I was rolling my things up, the guy across from my bed (Mitch) asked what I was doing. He was shocked when I said I was done living here. I really had nothing else to say except "See you." He sat there on his bunk looking at me. His mouth was open in disbelief. Other inmates were now lifting their heads from their pillows, watching in disbelief as I walked down the row.

Pushing the door wide open, I walked out of the Quonset hut letting the door slam for one last good-bye. I smiled, knowing I was headed for serious trouble.

After telling the guard I was done here, he looked at me in disbelief also. It was late and very quiet on the yard. They are usually short staffed on Sunday nights and didn't need a lot of guards to run the place.

They never put a guy like myself into the impossible equation that he'd role himself up on a Sunday night.

Then like an annoyed parent telling their child to get back into bed, he said, "I'm giving you a direct order to get back to your bunk now."

I moved closer to the window and looked him dead in the eye. "I'm done living here."

"Are you disobeying a direct order?"

"Yes," I said. All hell broke loose. He was on his radio yelling 10-16. I think the rush of adrenaline kind of blacked me out. This was serious.

Next thing I knew, two guards grabbed me and told me to get down on the ground. They handcuffed me and put me in a small holding room.

It was a four foot by three foot room with a wooden door. I sat in a chair against the wall. I had pulled my handcuffs from behind my back and under my legs to the front. They sure won't like that.

I could hear even more guards outside the door now and in somewhat of in a panic. This deal was getting bigger by the minute.

After about twenty minutes, they asked me again if I was disobeying a direct order. I told them again, "Yes."

There were twelve hands all fighting for a grip of me. It must have looked pretty silly seeing six men doing the job of one.

They knew I was not threatening and dangerous. I complied in every way. But they all want to be tough guys with their knees in my head and back. They're soft and out of shape. I'd be ashamed to be them. Imposters of justice.

We were raised young to honor this great country of ours. We were taught to respect those who fought for our liberty. We were told to trust those in authority and uniform. But these guys? I'd never.

It's saddening to have my freedom chained up by my own countrymen.

Living as "the bad guy" is one of the hardest things I have ever had to endure.

Prison and ex-con are just two words. A dishonorable title I will wear for the rest of my life.

What if Cindy would have been with me the night I crashed? What if I would of hurt, or even killed her?

I can't believe this is my life. What a waste of time. You only have so much life on this planet. To throw away even one minute is an atrocity.

These old boys just pulled me out of the holding room. They cuffed my handcuffs to a waist chain and put on tight leg shackles.

They walked me to the gate as the van pulled up. Time to go. As the van door was closing, I winked at the guy. Good riddance.

Breathing a sigh of relief, I leaned back in the seat. I felt more at peace already. Two guards sat quietly in the front. One driver and one shotgun man.

I could only see the side of his face in the dark shadows of the van. The shotgun guard was breathing heavy through his nostrils and kept glancing back at me. The way his hand was wrapped tight around the shotgun told me I wrecked his night of leisure.

Bouncing headlights shined through the mystery of the night leading us down the dusty road. The town is only about half an hour away. I enjoyed every second of that sweet, silent ride.

When we pulled up to the jail house, I was kind of stunned but smiled. It looked like an old Western jail house from the days of cowboys and gun fighters.

There were two sheriffs standing at the front doors. They welcomed me with a nod and half smile. The clang of the old steel bars closing told me good night.

There was nothing there but bars on the door. Nowadays most jails and prisons have solid steel doors.

I'm their only guest for the night. There is a folded blanket here on the end of my bunk, and it looks to be clean. I think I'll kick on back now and enjoy the peace of this place. I hear there's a storm coming through here tomorrow, and I'm in its path.

This one-man cell was good for me last night. I slept like a baby. I know it sounds weird, sleeping well in a jail cell, but it feels safe and secure to me. It's kind of primitive.

I was brought breakfast early this morning. It was from the local diner and pretty good. They gave me coffee, scrambled eggs, bacon, toast, and a carton of milk. Not a bad way to wake up.

That morning, they gave me some recreation time. The brick walls were twenty-five feet high, and the court floor is all smooth concrete. The sun was out but not directly shinning onto the court. It was nice out there in the fresh air.

Two other inmates came out for rec time. They were local friends from the next town over. Both had gotten into some trouble drinking a few nights before and were serving a four-day jail sentence.

Public indecency, peeing in the street that drunken night—they still thought it was funny. Leaning against the brick wall talking, they were proud and grinning about being in jail.

When they both ran out of wind talking about themselves, they asked me what I was in jail for. I said, "I'm in DOC custody. And I'm being transferred to super max."

Now looking like they just saw a ghost, one of them started pounding on the door. He was yelling, "Get us out of here! We're not supposed to be with him!"

The guards let the two out immediately. When he opened the door, these guys quickly slid past. The guard looked at me and shrugged his shoulders. Even locked up, there's people that think you're dangerous.

It's late morning, and I'm waiting to be transferred. I'll be going to the super max in Tucson. They'll reclassify me there for a new prison unit.

What do you know, it's school field trip day. Guess who's the main attraction. There's about fifteen second-graders walking past my cell. I can't believe this is happening. These are the last people in the world I want to see me as the bad guy.

They all walked past me slowly, never stopping and only about a foot away from my cell bars. Most of them glanced up at me quickly and then turned before my eyes could meet theirs. Some stared into my cell for a long time but only locked eyes for a moment. And then there were the little wide-eyed ones. They wouldn't dare turn their heads to look into my cell. They walked by all stiff-armed and straight-legged, frozen in fear.

I would have stayed seated as they passed but thought I'd give them what they came for. I grabbed the bars and looked through. I said nothing. It would be a better crime deterrent if I stayed mysterious. Keeping a straight face was hard, but the best thing I could have done for them.

I'm ready for transport. I hope my dad is not too upset when I'm finally able to call him. I've never thought how a father might feel about having a son locked up. I can only guess that it's a pretty helpless feeling to see my life pushed down like this.

TWENTY

Super maximum, super max, the hole, CDU (Central Detention Unit), or Lockdown. They're all the same no matter what you call it. I'm now at CDU. I arrived here early this afternoon. The ride was a nice one.

The sun seemed extra bright after staying in that dark cell. My eyes could reach far and wide breathing in the soft blue sky. Though my body was chained and inside that van, my eyes danced freely over the desert land. How sweet the sight with unrestricted light.

They (DOC) had me chained pretty tight today, knowing I was now a P&I, 5/5 score, the highest custody you can get. I was a 1/1 at my last unit, the lowest you can get, and now I'm 5/5. They will have to bring me down to at least a 5/4 to get me out of here and into max. Maybe they will make me a 4/4 and send me to Douglas. Douglas Prison is a high-medium security prison, which is just fine with me, except that it's the Siberia of the Arizona prison system. No one wants to go to Douglas—no one.

There are only troublemakers at Douglas. It's about five miles from the Mexican border and in the middle of nowhere. We have all heard of Douglas, and the stories are bad enough to scare even a convict.

We all know about the unit down there that was set on fire a couple of years ago. Some angry inmates torched the place good. The word gets around. Douglas is the place of forgotten inmates.

Besides Douglas prison being miles away from any societal accountability, it's also far from any penal accountability.

When you are at the worst prison in the system, you have nothing to lose. It's the prison ghetto down there.

When an inmate gets into trouble down in Douglas, they just keep you down there as your punishment. To go to any other prison would be a step up.

There is a high-medium unit and a low-medium unit down there. I also heard the high-medium unit has a split yard. That means they fenced off the yard cutting it in half to keep movement tightly confined after inmates tried to burn the unit down.

The high-medium unit has trailers on their yard for the inmates to live in. Temporary trailers. These are old single-wide trailers hooked together, making one long trailer for housing.

There are three or more of these long trailers per unit. There are rooms on both sides of the trailer, with long hallways splitting it down the middle. Each inmate has their own cell. All rooms have a window to the yard side or to the fence side.

There's about fifty rooms, plus a shower/bath room per trailer. I've heard that all the trailers have these incredibly long narrow hallways. Some inmates have been known to have bad "accidents" while walking down those dimly lit hallways. There are no guards down at the end of those long hallways either.

Guards and inmates all know that such a place inside a prison is basically a free for all.

The low-medium unit has open dorm living. After enduring the Quonset hut living, I don't dare try my patience with that again. I'd much rather live in ghetto trailers and dangerous hallways.

I've heard guys say it's difficult to get a guard to work there. They send a lot of the misfit guards there as an ultimatum to being fired. You just know the cream of the crop is not working down there.

For others, I've heard that DOC will promote them up to the rank of sergeant within the prison system, just to get someone to work down there. With that kind of promotion, their pay scale is much higher.

If every guard down there at Douglas is the rank of sergeant, then who's in charge. The inmates are.

There's nothing to do down there. No schooling or library. It's just an open yard with a weight pile. The gun towers stand ready, while inmates sit idle.

Well, enough of that talk. Man, this CDU place is as tight as a drum. You don't even move in this place without a two guard escort. I'm on the bottom tier in a two-man cell. David is my cellmate, but he's not the same David from Santa Cruz.

There is no inmate movement inside here, only the guards go from cell to cell. This unit is a 24-7 lockup. You have one half hour for a shower every other day, and you have one half hour in the dog pen every other day.

Inmates at CDU are well-seasoned and come from throughout the prison system. No one would dare yell anything disrespectful as you are walked into your cell.

There was an inmate up on the second tier that was one of my cellmates from the maximum unit. His name is John, and that's the first I've seen of him in almost two years. You don't forget the guys you started your time with.

On the bottom tier was a guy from Santa Cruz, Jeff. I only knew him in passing, but he was cool. In a place like this, it's best to know people. We hold a mutual respect for each other.

Danny was the top AB man on Santa Cruz yard. He and I acknowledged each other on the yard, but never talked other than that. He did his thing, and he let me do mine. I say let me do mine because he held the power to make my life difficult. He found no reason to make me friend nor foe. Nor I him.

This is the first unit I have ever seen the color blue. All the other units, from the jail house to here, have all been either gray or sage green. They say that the color is to keep the inmates calm. I don't know about calm, but it will sure depress you. This place is very clean, bright, and well kept.

Security in this unit is extremely high. Before an inmate is taken from his cell, the inmate must first be handcuffed through the hand-shackle door.

You go through this every time you leave your cell. The thing is, after a while, it's just the norm and can be done in just about thirty seconds. It's only the fish guards that stumble and make it take longer than it should.

Here I sit in a prison cell, just as ordered. I'm fine with a cell-mate. Being that you don't get your TV or radio in the hole, I've at least got someone to talk and play cards with. We're just passing the time in here. Remember, there's no such thing as time in here.

I've been here most of the day. I know this because it's getting dark outside. We can't really see the outside from our cell, though you can see the outside light through the door. We have no windows going to the outside. Highest security gets you a room with no view.

Our cell is the last cell on the end. There are about ten cells to our right, and there are about ten cells to our left. We sit in the corner. There is also the second tier just above us.

The shower is a one-man shower they lock you into just like a cell. It's about a four by four room. When you go from cell to shower, they chain you up. Hands, waist, and legs. It's literally two small steps from my cell. They let me shower soon after I arrived here. After you're done showering, you pound on the door and wait. What a pain.

I met the guy in the cell to our left as I was getting in the shower. He said they call him Mickey, and he's been here for months. He seemed like a nice enough guy and just wanted some news from whatever yard he could get it from. That's how it works here; we pass the news from yard to yard.

After I got back into the cell, David gave me the lowdown on Mickey. He talked pretty softly as he was telling me about why Mickey was here in the hole. A few months ago, Mickey helped kill a guy over on another yard. Everyone knew about it.

Here in Tucson, like other prisons, there are more than one yard per prison.

Anyway Mickey and two other inmates took care of this white guy over there. Some dumb "white guy" was helping some "nonwhite guys" collect on a debt one day. Mickey and some other guys got wind of this and went and made an example out of him.

Mickey and two others set it up so as to catch this guy in the open yard, in front of the whole yard. I guess this man never saw it coming.

The three of them casually walked over to this guy in the yard and encircled him. Before he knew it, they started stabbing him. When he realized what was happening, it was too late. Hitting the dirt with wide eyes, he stopped moving. They turned away and left him there bleeding.

It happened so fast that the gun towers didn't have time to respond. But then they quickly had the three of them in their scope sights until cuffed and taken away.

Mickey came into prison with a six-year sentence, and now he will never leave. The other two guys were both already doing twenty-five to life for their crimes and will also for sure never leave.

That's my only real fear here in prison, doing something that keeps me here longer or maybe even for life. Prison is unpredictable. Anything could happen before you get to the gate.

I know that just above our cell on the second tier is an inmate that was on death row. I don't know how that all works. On death row, and then not? I don't think Arizona has the death penalty right now. Prison is full of dangerous people, so to be safe, you better be dangerous.

I've got to say, this place makes more sense to me than that little boys camp they had me at. These guys in here don't scare me like I thought they would. They're just like me, and I'm just like them. I know that sounds funny. Don't hurt me, or I'll hurt you back. Let me do my time, and I'll let you do yours. Unspoken law.

Cool, looks like we can get mail here in the hole. The guard is going from cell to cell doing mail-call right now. I'm hoping Cindy has finally sent me letter. Nope. Well, I think I'll write to my mom today. I always write to her letting her know I'm doing fine. I try and put her at ease. I don't want her to worry or get sad about me being in here.

My dad, I can tell him everything. I think he can handle it well because he's a guy. It would break my mom's heart knowing her son is getting hard hearted. I just tell her I'm eating well and working out.

She knows I can take care of myself. I always just tell her I'm doing fine, and that's it. I love her way to much too ever let her see the pain inside my heart from being locked away in here.

TWENTY ONE

It's been over two months, and I'm still here. They have told me they're going to send me to central unit. That's the "walls," the last place I want to be. It's the max unit in Florence, and I'm scared to go down there as a short timer.

I've only got about a year left to do before I'll be paroling out. That's short time, and most guys down there are doing life. It's kind of like I've done my hard time. I don't want to go back to the front lines again at this stage of the game.

A lot of guys say it's great down there because there's drugs at that unit. I know that DOC is trying to hit me back hard for rolling myself up.

I was brought outside and put into the dog cage the other day, and Danny was in the cage across from me. We both said our gentlemanly "Hey now," and he turned back to the old-timer in the cage next to him and kept talking. The old-timer said nothing to me except a quick silent nod upward with his head, in which I respectfully returned back.

The "dog cage" is just what it sounds like. That's where we go for our recreation time. It's nothing more than two rows of individual chain-link fence cages on both sides of the walkway. It's just like the dog pound. It's enough room so you can walk around in circles and do pushups. It's really nice to have some fresh air because living in a small prison cell twenty-four hours a day with another man can get pretty stuffy.

You are totally encaged out here. Concrete flooring and chain link. The cool thing is seeing the sunlight. Sky is all you'll see above, and rows of inmates are all you'll see across from you.

Danny turns my direction as I'm exercising and says, "Hey, Merk [my nick name]. I hear you're going down to central unit?"

"Yeah, but I really don't want to."

"You'll like it there. I'm heading there also. They're some great guys over there, and you'll do just fine."

What Danny did next blew my mind. He looked to the old-timer in the cage next to him saying, "Hey, Merk, this is Billy. Billy, this is Merk and he's okay."

We both simultaneously gave each other a nod. With Danny's next breath, he turned to Billy, "Give Merk your smokes."

Without hesitation, Billy slid a brand new pack of cigarettes under the cage to me. It didn't matter if I smoked or not. This was a sign of respect, from Danny to me. I was completely shocked.

Seeing Billy move without hesitation showed how much power Danny holds. "Billy just got done doing twenty-five years. He's a good soldier," Danny said. "He's getting out in a few days, and we're going to miss him."

"Yeah, I can imagine that, Danny." Sincerely smiling, I nodded, thanking them both for the smokes.

I was being removed from my cage by the officers as we were finishing our conversation. "Take care, Billy, and thanks again, Danny, I appreciate it." They both gave me a nod as I was walking away and being escorted back to my cell.

I could see that the guards that were chaining me up and walking me out had a certain type of respect for these two guys. I'm not sure how I knew it, but I could just feel it on them.

I always knew Danny had been watching me on the other yard, directly or indirectly. He knows that I mind my own business and walk softly.

This whole thing showed me the power this guy carries. Maybe he wants me to know that I've got somewhere to go, if I ever cross the tracks. For whatever the reason, I was now acknowledged among the kin of prison gladiators.

Wham! There it is right on time. It's late-night count, and the guards here are like the guards elsewhere. Flashlight in the eyes. I saw David get hit with it, as we both turned our heads. We all know that the light is a nontangible item. But it's still a visible invasion of our space. Fighting with the guards about proper flashlight etiquette is as futile as trying to beat your opponent at shadow boxing.

We play a lot of cards in here, only because there's nothing else to do. Sleep or cards is what's on the daily itinerary, every day. Sometimes we'll do a deck of cards for pushups. It's like this: Take a deck of cards and flip over the top card, whatever the card is that's how many pushups you have to do. You take turns after each card. I know, simple. Do that a few times, and you'll start feeling it. Whoever can't do what his card says loses. This is the one game I never lose at, never.

Though I wish I could say the same about other card games. David kept beating me at spades, so I told him, if he won one more game, I was going to kick his ass. He knew I was serious and folded his hand.

We didn't play cards for a few days after that little breakdown of mine. I think I'm getting a bit stir crazy after being in here for a few months. Sometimes this place is like a pressure cooker, if you're taken out on time you're going to be pretty tender, but if they leave you in for too long, you're going to be tough.

There are quite a few inmates at CDU that are overcooked. You can hear them yelling and pounding on their doors day and night, demanding this and that. "Wake up, boys, don't you know where you're at. We're sick of your whining and don't want to hear your sissy crying anymore."

It seem as if there's always at least one jerk who's trying to get more than what he's got coming. Like one minute its "I didn't get a regular-size portion of food in my tray, and I want another tray." Or "My milk was sour. Give me another." Or "I need more toilet paper." And my favorite one is "I'm supposed to have a legal call. When do I get my legal call. I'm supposed to meet with my lawyer, and I need to call and find out when I'm supposed to meet with him."

Over and over, they complain about what they're not getting. I actually kind of feel sorry for the guards when they have to keep dealing with these idiots.

The whole lawyer thing really cracks me up. I laugh my butt off about that one. I'm thinking to myself, *Dang, bro, you should have thought about talking to your lawyer a long time ago. I don't think there's a lawyer alive that want's to jump inside this fire with you.*

But to be serious, some of these guys here at CDU have committed new crimes while inside of prison and they do need an attorney for the new charges against them.

I'll bet Mickey has a legal visit coming to him pretty soon if not already. When an inmate commits a new crime inside of prison, they go through the whole legal process all over again. It's just as if they were out on the street and committed the crime. Sooner or later, they send the accused inmate back to the Phoenix jail and start balancing the scales of justice once again.

Let's go "fishing." That's what we call passing things from cell to cell. If an inmate wants to give me some tobacco or whatever, how's he going to get that to me when he's eight cells down.

My fishing equipment was invented long ago by inmates of ingenuity. Only two items are required in your tackle box: a magazine and string. The longer the string, the better. Anybody can have a magazine, but string is hard to come by.

String can be made of many different things. Bed sheets, pillowcases, T-shirts, socks, or any fabric you have access too. After tying all the string together into one long line, you are ready to go fishing.

You need about fifteen feet of string. Now having the magazine lassoed around the center pages, and the string line coming off the bottom like a tail, close the magazine and the lasso is not coming off.

Fishing is a little tricky at first, for a fish. Hold the string in one hand and slide the magazine under your cell door and to the cell door you are targeting. Sliding with speed and accuracy is hard.

Holding the magazine by its spine, you flick it under your door. That's how it's done. Don't forget to hold the string tight, or else you'll lose it all.

Sometimes it takes two inmates to correctly dial in the accuracy of the launch coordinate. Once the magazine hits the bull's-eye, they have only a little minute to load the cargo. A speedy extraction is required.

The payload is always in the center of the magazine and should be pulled back swiftly but cautiously, so as not to lose your fresh catch. Sometimes the guards see this and sometimes not. It depends if they're in the control room or out in the pod. They'll try to intercept, sometimes, if they suspect it's contraband.

Otherwise it's no big deal to them. Though technically we're not supposed to "fish," they'll let us do it. That's so they're not playing errand boy when we ask them to give something to another inmate. We are allowed to share certain items; it's the transporting that's hard.

They brought a new guy into CDU earlier today and put him into Mickey's cell. To say that Mickey is just a little upset would be a huge understatement. The new guy is not having much of a welcoming party. If you can imagine, a young clean-cut skinny guy with no tattoos and the street-smarts of a senator's kid, then you can imagine the trouble George (the new guy) has just stepped into.

Mickey has already told George he can't stay there and that he needs to find a new cell by day's end. The stress is beaming from George's eyes like an SOS. He's desperately looking out into the open sea of the pod and hoping the rescue party will spot him before his boat submerges completely.

Though unaware, I was to become the lighthouse within this frightening storm of his. Guiding him through the thick fog and into safe harbor could prove itself challenging.

I've already talked a little with George today. Their door is only a few feet away from ours. After seeing him peer through the window with wide eyes shortly after arriving, I introduced myself. George wasted no time telling me about his dilemma.

"This guy says I won't wake up in the morning." His voice moved toward me like an oversized wave, smooth and steady at first, then bursting like thunder, crashing and spilling everywhere.

George was losing his composure quickly. "You're going to be fine. Don't panic just relax. Tell Mickey to come to the door."

"Hey, Mick, what's going on, bro?"

"Nothing, Paul, I just don't want this kid in my cell. He's a fish and clueless."

"I've got a sharp toothbrush." He shrugged his shoulders and returned back to his bunk. Dang, he just wants a reason to kill somebody.

As Mickey was going back to his bunk, George was coming back to the window again. It was strange talking to them through the window as if the other person wasn't there.

He was at his door window again, big eyed. "Paul, you've got to help me, please! Talk to him Paul, please talk to him."

"Look here, George, you need to tell the guards to move you. That's what you need to do. You need to stay calm and tell them that you don't feel safe inside that cell and that they need to move you now."

George only now needs to convince DOC that his life is actually 100 percent in danger, and that it's not just about two cellmates not getting along. I told George to get Mickey to the window.

"Hey, Mick, be cool and give this kid a chance, will ya. You don't want all that on your soul. He'll get out of there soon."

In just short of a whisper, he said, "Okay, Paul, soon."

"Thanks, I appreciate that Mick."

Shortly after, George flagged down the first guard walking into our pod. The guard had his is ear pressed on their window so he could hear George's plea. I nodded to the guard as he was listening, as if to say, get him out of there.

George was now trying to be a little more discreet in the plot that griped him. Though other inmates overheard us earlier, he didn't want to look afraid now.

DOC removed George from Mickey's cell shortly after that talk with the guard and transferred him out to a new pod. I leaned close into my window as the officers were taking George out of the cell and reassured him there was no shame in asking to be moved.

Relieved and looking through my window, he said, "Thanks, Paul." I wished him well as he turned and walked out, never looking back. Mickey laid low for a few days after, and we saw nothing of him.

We all have our fears in prison just as in the free world. What scares me might not scare you, and what scares you might not scare me. If you're the kind of guy that says you're never afraid, then you're not telling the truth. Some guys are afraid of getting out of prison and living in the free world. Some guys are afraid of staying in prison and never seeing the free world.

We all have fears. The only thing I've ever found to help me with fear is faith. Faith is like love; you can only see love when it's in action.

I can see that this prison is trying hard to drown me. The depth is disorientating me. I'm trying hard to find my way back to the surface for a much-needed breath.

Everyone cries sometimes. Remember what I said before about "being in prison, but don't let the prison be in you." I'm trying so hard to keep this prison out of me. Some days, it seems it's seeped into my very pores, and rigor mortis has started to set in.

I'm getting hardhearted and cynical. God help me to get back to who I was before I came here. This war and its battles are saturating my spirit and drowning me.

I feel forgotten after being here month after month. No letters from anyone. They say it takes longer to get letters in the hole, but I'm still mad anyway. My heart aches.

During my outside time today, I glanced up at the afternoon sky. It was refreshingly clear. The powder blue color was smiling at me in the same way a summertime swimming pool entices you to jump into it.

As I'm submerged, I think . . . There are at least a million other places on the planet I could be right now. But I'm here in this dog pen.

I chose to drive my car after drinking. It's that simple. I chose one night, over many sunny days. One night cost myself this sunny day and all the others that I'll never get back. What about all those summer nights I've missed out on. I thought something like this could never happen to a guy like me. God, what a high price to pay. It took only one night to put a never-ending lifetime mortgage on my life.

TWENTY TWO

Finally, they moved me out of CDU. I've really fallen down into the pit of the prison system. It's true, they've sent me into Siberia! Well, not the real Siberia, but its equivalent geographically. Though it is the extreme opposite in temperature and terrain, I am sure the suffering is sufficiently the same.

I am now in Douglas, Arizona. I will most likely be here until my sentence is completed. DOC rolled us up early in the morning. It was about 4:30 a.m. when they came pounding on our cell doors. We were on the prison bus about a half hour later.

You're adrenaline starts pumping through you like a caveman. These guys are pretty hardcore in CDU and just because we are all chained up doesn't mean someone can't get hurt.

There were about twenty-five of us on the bus. Our first and only stop was here at the Douglas Prison. I think just about every one of us got off of the bus here at the high-medium unit side.

It's just a wasteland out here. Crazy how they put this massive prison in the middle of nowhere. There's nothing around for miles. It's the Arizona desert in every direction. It's so hot and dry, you can even see the heat waves out in the distance.

I'm sure it's got its share of rattlesnakes and lizards slithering around out there amongst all that cactus, desert brush, and tumble-weeds. They say the Mexican border is only about seven miles away from here. That could be one heck of a fun run. But then what? It's just more of the same on that side of the border.

I can't begin to tell you how wonderful it feels to be out of super max after being locked down 24-7 for three and a half months.

I am locked down tight in the middle of no civilization. If I screamed, would anyone hear me?

This yard is laid out much different than the other prison yards. DOC split this yard into two separate yards after the inmates put a torch to the place a couple of years ago.

They drove us straight to the prison yard and not into some administration building, like they usually would have.

There is a prison yard on our left side and on our right side. This road between the two yards is just wide enough for the bus to drive through. Each yard is a little over one hundred yards long.

The bus stopped at about the middle of these two prison yards, at the main gates. They split the yard down the middle with the dirt road and fence. DOC made this yard change after the riot for better inmate control.

When I was getting off the bus, the guard told me to go on the right side yard, and Dave, my cellmate, was told to go to the left side yard.

He and I were chained together on the bus ride. We had no problem going in different directions after those long months together. We get along just fine, but it's a lot of time to spend with one person. A road trip with your best friend can get a little edgy; try a prison cell. Eating, sleeping, and bathroom, 24-7. We were happy in parting ways.

Prison is confinement. Sometimes you're in a small space, and sometimes, in a large space. But both are confinement. A very hard adjustment to reality. Let the time tick . . .

It's been a few months since I've been at Douglas. Maybe I've been here a thousand years and don't know it yet. Maybe I've been living in the same day for a hundred years. My calendar lies to me, telling me every day is still only today. Who knows the time? This is a fairytale word, from a fairytale land, of a story told long ago . . .

My new place is not so bad. I'm in a trailer at the far end of the yard. The prison yard is outlined in prisoner housing.

There was a schoolhouse on the yard before they burned the building down. It's all boarded up and not used for anything.

The weight pile is in the middle of the yard. The basketball court is to the left of that. And the dirt running track encircles the yard.

The other yard is through the main gate. They keep a guard there but usually don't say a thing as you cross through. That yard has a sand volleyball court and a track, but no weight pile. It does have the kitchen and chow hall also. There is a small chapel on the far end, along with maintenance and inmate store. Our yard houses more inmates. They lose housing room with the kitchen and other buildings over there.

There are about eight hundred or so inmates between both yards. I feel that DOC is a little scared of this place, and they should be. There is not a lot of room at central unit where most of us should be. I think they save that place for really hardcore new guys until they settle into the system and calm down a bit. So the hardcore guys that are not showing complete uncontrollability can be housed down here at Douglas.

There are some guys here doing big time, ten, fifteen, twenty-plus years.

I'm settling into my new house, and I'm not complaining. It's a single-man cell. I'm about halfway down the dimly lit hallway and that puts me pretty close to the bathroom. But not too close as to hear the noise from inside. There are lots of loud mouths and slamming doors. And the smell could kill a grizzly bear.

My cell has a solid metal door. It has a ten-by-ten-inch square window at the top. The cell itself is only an eight-by-eight-foot, but that's good because it's all mine.

It's basically just a bunk and built-in desk. It has a little wall next to that to hang up clothes and put your state-issued fishnet bag. Your dirty clothes can be sent out to laundry once a week, and they go by way of your fishnet bag, which has your name and prison number on it.

At Santa Cruz, I paid the laundry guy a pack of smokes every week to do my wash the right way. No starch. Dried completely.

Folded nicely. After getting my clothes back the first few times, I went and worked out our laundry deal.

In my entire life, I have never seen such a disgusting bathroom. It's the inmates that choose to live like this. And DOC says nothing about it.

Soap scum, toothpaste, and shaving stubble cover the countertops. It's been there for quite some time.

The taste of the air over the sinks enters your lungs as if something died and decomposed in the drains. It targets your gagging reflex uncontrollably, as you're brushing your morning teeth.

That first day, I covered my mouth in amazement and disgust, but the flavor of the room had already overwhelmed my senses. I walked quickly down the hallway and out the unit door for some overdue untouched air.

After wiping my watering eyes and convincing my lungs they were safe again, I went over to the next unit and finished.

There it is again. Late-night count. My eyes just had their daily optometrist appointment. My fault, I should know better by now and turned my head.

TWENTY THREE

I've been working in the kitchen ever since I arrived. I had one foot in the door because of the year I did at Santa Cruz's kitchen. I always received the highest work evaluations, which proved valuable when I came looking for this job.

They put me to work on one of the five flat grills. I fry eggs every morning. I love it. Sunny side up, over easy, over hard, and broke yoke over hard. After I'm done cooking, I cook up a few for myself.

I eat one dozen eggs over easy, toast, hash browns, grits, and a few glasses of milk every morning. Then I'll take my half-hour morning walk. It's a great way to start my day.

My workouts are pretty hard, and I burn a lot of calories. I'm on the weight pile twice a day, and my running is back up at two hours a day. My weigh-ins are a solid 225 lbs every week. I'm in prime shape.

Though the gladiator stands ready and willing, he himself never opens the arena gate.

Today was the day. I've had enough of this guy and his bull dog stares at me. Almost every day for the last month, this guy gives me a real hard-ass look. He's a big corn fed boy from somewhere out of state. I don't know what his problem is with me, but I'm going to find out.

My buddy Johnny tells me I'm crazy if I think I'm going to go down and talk to this guy. Johnny's a good friend I met about six months ago, just after I hit the yard. He's as funny as they come and a pretty nice guy all around. He's kind of a small guy, so when he pumps his chest out big and says, "Come on and get yourself some," it's pretty funny. He knows he's not that big, but he can definitely handle himself.

Johnny's in for a pretty long stretch. I think seventeen years. He stabbed a cop one night when he thought the cop was going to shoot him. The cop lived, but it was pretty bad. Johnny's my age, and he still has about ten more years to do.

He's a good brother of mine, that's for sure. We talk about all the real stuff in life—God, family, staying on the right course, and our futures after prison. It seems every now and then, God puts a good friend in your life just when you need it. I can count on one hand the friends He has put in my life through the years. That might not seem like a lot. But for me, just one is a lot.

Friendship is not family, and family is not friendship. Though in friendship, you choose whose blood you will honor, and in family, you honor the blood that was chosen.

Anyway, this guy keeps looking at me all hard and crazy every time I pass him. He's about six feet seven inches tall and about 275 lbs. Not a small guy, but that's not the point.

The point is he's a white guy that's not affiliated with any organization. There's no backlash or others to think about when confronting this guy. If he was a part of something, then I'd really have to rethink approaching him, but he's not.

He's a seasoned convict that's been around the block. He walks confidently, but he's uncaring as to what others might be feeling. He's either thinking I'm some kind of punk that wouldn't dare to say anything, or he's just looking for a fight. Either way, I'm your man. For whatever the reason, we're now all going to find out.

After work, I went to my house and took off my T-shirt and tightened my boot laces. This guy lives at the last door all the way at the end of my unit hallway. It's pretty dark down there and far enough away from the entrance doors that no one should ever see or hear us from the outside. That also means that my exit is pretty far away if this guy hurts me. Though in the moment, I'm not thinking about this at all.

I'm ready. I start walking toward his cell. For some reason, I'm calm before this battle begins. The last time I fought a guy this big, I had some ribs broken, but I don't see that happening today.

Every day inside of prison is a risk. At any time, day or night, things can happen that change a person's life forever. No one is safe from this reality. This is true in the free world too, but you have many more emergency exits.

As he looks me in the eye through the window of his door, I see disdain on his face. He opens the door and sits, clueless that he has called the war.

He said, "What's up, Holmes?"

His eyes widen, and his posture stiffens. The uncontrollable physical reaction of fight or flight has taken control.

"What's up is I want to know if you and I have got a problem? Seems to me you keep looking at me hard in the hallway." I stood, waiting for his reply of flying fists and fury, but neither came.

"No, bro, we're cool. I'm just real short and waiting to hit the gate. I'm a little uptight waiting and all, but I didn't mean anything by it. We're all cool, Holmes . . . My name is Al."

"Hey, Al, my name is Paul. I just kept thinking you had it in for me, and I couldn't figure out why."

"Hey, Paul. No, I don't have it in for ya, but don't worry about it, I understand." Then Al asked if I wanted to come in and have some coffee. We sat for about half an hour talking and drinking coffee in his cell.

He turned out to be a pretty cool guy. Al's from the state of Florida and had not been home for over fifteen years. He pulled an armed robbery back in the day when he had a drug problem. He got fifteen years flat and was now days away from being released. "Flat time" means you do all of the years you are sentenced to with no good time early release.

It never ceases to amaze me how life can turn around in a split second. One minute, I'm going to fight with this guy, and the next second, I'm having coffee with him. It's crazy.

I sure am glad that one's gone off my plate. This yard feels more desperate and dangerous than the Santa Cruz yard. I think it's just because we're so far away from the real world.

The tension is very real here. I know it's got a lot to do with the lack of visits. Phoenix is about four hours away, very rarely does someone get a visit here at Douglas. No love coming in means no love going out. There's some real haters on this yard.

A few weeks ago on the basketball court, some jerk I don't even know got all tough guy with me. Johnny, myself, and a few others I know were goofing around on the court playing a little "contact" basketball. Some guy I've never even seen thought he could just jump in the game and start banging me around.

I got pretty upset and told this guy he'd better back off and take a walk. He thought his out of shape old ass was going to have a banner day when he said, "Let's go on the other side of that burned-out building, and I'll kick your ass."

I looked at that lazy slug, and I told him, "Let's do it right here, right now."

He stood there holding the ball. "I'm not fighting in front of the gun towers and risk getting shot."

"I don't care about some gun towers. I'm not walking over there to fight you. Let's do it here. And don't even think about throwing that ball in my face."

He mumbled something and dropped the ball. He turned and walked away with cussing words under his breath.

This guy is a real bad apple. I'll be glad to meet up with him later if he likes. I don't have much sympathy for weaklings trying to make themselves feel good by trying to make someone else feel bad.

TWENTY FOUR

Running from the dogs. That's what DOC has asked me to do. There's an inmate that's getting out soon, and his job is to run from the dogs. DOC trains their tracking hound dogs a few times a week by having them track an inmate out into the desert.

The sergeant on my yard asked me if I'd put in for the job. He said that my classification will be going down soon, and I would qualify for the job then. He said he's seen me running for the last few mouths and thought I'd be great for the job. He said I'd get moved to the "porters yard," which is a great yard for guys with lower P&I scores that become "trustees" at the prison. You get to live in the best housing unit there is.

Private living quarters are cleaner and quieter. Only twelve trustees on the whole "closed yard," which means no other inmate contact. Better food along with daily store privileges and much better pay. I get 25 cents an hour right now working in the kitchen. If I run, I'll make 75 cents. I'd also get more freedom on the closed yard, and I'd get to stay out later at night.

I told the sergeant I'd need to think about it and then let him know. I'll have to think about this for sure, even though right now it sounds like heaven compared to this place.

It kind of feels like I'd be a traitor to the other inmates if I'm working for DOC. But then again, I'm not choosing to be a bad guy like some of them. It would put me right in the middle of both guard and inmate. Half inmate. Half guard.

The dog running job puts me on the outside of the fence. DOC would give me about a half-hour head-start before they would track me. That could be a lot of fun, running out there in the open desert. I'm afraid I could out run those dogs, and then what happens?

I had the prison baker ask me a few days ago if I'm happy cooking in the mornings. He said that he bakes all night long for the prison and is looking for a helper to take the job of his old assistant who just made parole.

The job is night work, and we'd be the only one's there. I'd get to sleep in the day and work at night. The pay is 50 cents an hour, and the work only takes about half the night to do. You get to lounge around the other half of the night and still get paid for it. He said the job is a great one, and you don't have to see all the other convicts during the day because you're sleeping. At night, everyone is locked down, so you have the place to yourself.

Two job offers that both sound pretty good. Johnny has also told me that if I ever wanted to work in the maintenance department, he'd get me in for sure. He does carpentry for the prison because he was a house framer in the free world.

It's been almost a year since I've had visitors. The minimum unit was too far away for getting many visits, so I had only a few. Way down here in "Siberia," I'm not going to get any.

I know Cindy's slowly letting go, and I understand. I wish she'd just say it's over. All that she's really said is I'm getting "hard hearted."

I think I'll take the night job as assistant baker. I need to just keep to myself and get through this last year. I need to get on down the road before something bad happens in here.

If I take the running job, I'll be in the spotlight, and that's the last thing I want. There is too much pain inside myself, and when I'm around other people, it makes it hurt even more. God, get me out of here. I really can't take too much more. Three summers have passed. And soon three Christmases.

I wouldn't wish this on Anybody. But if Anybody drinks and drives, then Anybody could live here.

Be Somebody . . . Don't let Anybody drink and drive.

I've been baking for about a month and a half. I kind of like it. My daily routine is different, and my sleep pattern is messed up, but it's cool.

It's surreal staying up throughout the night. And it's peaceful without any inmates in sight. Amnesia is your blanket for the night. We'll even open the back door sometimes as we're working in the heat. Feeling the cool night air brush across my face awakens memories of some other place. The summers of my past are affectionately attached.

Late nights have allowed me to ponder the dreams of my future. It's in the acceptance of my dreams that I find challenging. Be who you really are, and destiny will come calling.

My routine is still much the same as far as workouts and eating goes. I don't hang out playing cards and drinking coffee at night like I used to with Johnny and a few other guys. Johnny and I still walk the track after dinner, talking and joking around. I don't work the weekends either so he and I will sometimes chill out playing backgammon. Really not that much to do on this yard.

I'm up for parole next month, but I'm not holding my breath. They took about two months "good time" from me, for rolling myself up from that mirage of a minimum unit. I think it works like this: For every two days I do in prison, I get one day (good time) off my sentence. That's how DOC calculates your parole date, and how much time you'll be on parole once you're out of prison.

I've seen guys in here fight with DOC for years about how much "good time" they should actually have and how DOC has incorrectly calculated their release date. I guess there is an actual formula that they use to determine your good time and release date.

As I'm thinking about not getting out until they say so, I'm reminded of one other way you can get out of prison without them saying so. The other way is from not breathing. Some guys get out of prison by someone else's hand. Some guys get out of here by their own hand.

About three weeks ago, I was coming from my yard over to the other yard. I was on my way to the chow hall for lunch on a Sunday afternoon. It was pretty hot outside for November, but then again, it is Douglas, Arizona.

There were not too many guys outside because of the heat. Most inmates rest up in their cells on the weekends. There is always at least one guard that stands at the gate checking inmates, as we move from one yard to the other.

Remember, there is a dirt road the divides the two yards. When a truck needs to pass between the two yards, the guard either closes the two main gates or just tells everyone to hold back until the truck passes.

I'm walking up to the gate that day, and the guard yells over at two other inmates and myself to hold up and wait. The guard is across the road at the other gate entrance, and he stops inmates on that side as well. To my left, I see this big dump truck that was just let inside the gates. And it's coming our way up the road. To my amazement, I look up at the driver and see a friend from Santa Cruz driving that big dump truck toward us.

It was Larry. Sometimes he and I would walk the track talking. He was the guy some inmates didn't like me talking with. I waved at him. I didn't know he was at Douglas. He must be at the minimum if he's driving.

With one inmate standing on my left and one on my right. I looked up at Larry as he's passing.

"How you doing, Paul?"

"Good, Larry, how you doing?"

At that moment, the back end of the truck lifted a few feet.

As Larry was hitting the brakes to see what just happened, I was looking at the old man that was standing to my left, except for now, he was under the dump truck and lying on the ground. This guy of maybe seventy years decided he was done with prison life and life altogether. He dove headfirst under the dump truck wheels.

I saw it out of the corner of my eye, but my brain just didn't want to believe what it was seeing. Larry stopped the truck and jumped out. He walked around the back, and the guard came over with him. Both looked shocked to see this old guy wedged under the back tires.

I heard the guard yelling something on his radio, and then it was on the yard speaker almost instantly. "Lockdown! Lockdown! Code Red lockdown! Everyone back to your cells." They closed the yard fast and had the medics on site quickly.

We knew this guy was gone, just from the way he was lying there lifeless. The dump truck was loaded down with a few tons of dirt.

It made me kind of sad to think this old guy had to go out this way. Who knows what kind of emotional or physical pain he must have been in. This was his only way out of it all. I can understand wanting to check out sometimes, but there is much in life I still want to see and do. What do they say about not judging a man unless you first walk a mile in his shoes? That saying fits this old man just fine. Yes, RIP, old man, RIP.

The first month I was here at Douglas, I almost took a razor blade and cut open my eyebrows. Why would anyone do such a thing? Pain. I had the worst sinus infection in the world. My sinuses hurt so bad with pressure that I thought that cutting them open was the only way to relieve the pain. DOC thought I could just tough it out for almost five days.

We've got some real jerk guys in here. Some inmates fake it. They're bored with life and need a little attention. They make the line five days long for a guy like me.

Those where some tough shoes to walk in. I thank God that help finally came my way. DOC acts as if every inmate is a liar. They are so afraid of getting fooled and looking bad.

Okay, I get it, this place has some really bad people, but at least, use some common sense sometimes. If a guy looks like his pain is out of this world, maybe it is.

It's as if all the ones that were beat up on the schoolyard as kids are now sadistically paying it back to the one's that remind them of their tormentors from long ago.

Prison, the wasteland of the world. The ones taking out the trash and keeping the dump in order act as if their lives are without sin or whatever word makes you feel more comfortable.

The next time one of you guards feel like looking down your nose at one of us in here, think about those dirty little secrets that you own. They might not all be illegal within the laws of our land, but you know in your heart that they are just as damaging to your soul.

TWENTY FIVE

I love December in Arizona. It's always sunny and in the seventies. Johnny and I just got done on the weight pile, and we're heading over to the mail room.

I've been waiting a long time to hear from Cindy. I sent her a letter about a month ago and nothing back as of yet. She sent me one of those short but sweet letters last time, like a quick note to say she was fine. I know she started back at school in August and has been busy with work. I understand the infrequency of letters. But I think I'm about due.

Johnny just got a letter from his ex-wife, and that means it's from his daughter. He's told me how his wife was pregnant when he came to prison. She divorced him soon after but still brings his little girl to visit, sometimes.

I've never seen such pain on one man as when Johnny talks about his little girl growing up without him. It hurts my heart to feel that sadness for both of them. There are some really heart-wrenching happenings in this world of ours. Like the sorrow of a little one missing their parent and a parent missing their little one.

There is nothing on this planet more pure and innocent than the heart of a child. One bad choice and here we are, and there they are. Separate lives, in separate dimensions. One lives in a place of time and space. And one lives in a place of no time and no space. Neither one understands the other.

Life does not know death, and death does not know life. The two cannot coexist in the same breath. Life knows only life, and death knows only death. They meet only in passing. They never commingle.

I got a letter from Cindy. And a letter from my dad who writes me pretty religiously, and I him. The shocker is this letter from Cindy. I can't seem to smell her perfume on it though. She always puts a dab or two on her letters. Maybe it's in the middle of the letter, and that's why I can't smell it yet.

Johnny's on his way to his cell to read his letters, and I'm heading to my house to read mine. My dad has put some more money on my books, so I'm able to hit the store again this week (thanks, Dad), and he says all is well with him and the family.

My dad has stayed close to me ever since I've been in prison, and it means a lot to me. He's never put me down or scolded me for my crash. He know's I've done enough of that to myself. He just tells me he's proud of me for who I am and that I'll make good of my life when I'm out of prison. My dad is always encouraging me and letting me know he's with me no matter what. He's a very honorable father, and I love him a lot.

I'm hesitant to open Cindy's letter. Yes, I'm a little scared to let her touch my heart. It might just all fall apart. Her words of tenderness were all it used to take to focus me on some other time and some other place. I'm not sure when and how, but my heart has become callous now. She's asleep within my soul where it's still safe, only in my nighttime dreams does she become wide-awake.

> Dear Paul, my sweet loving Paul. I know it's been a long time in writing you. Please forgive me. I really want you to know I love you, Paul, and the times we have spent together will always be in my heart. I miss you so very much. Every day my heart speaks to me of our distance and asks for relief, but none comes to it. I miss so many things about you, Paul, that I'm not sure where to even begin. My heart

aches for you as the sun aches to shine on a cold and rainy day. You are, and always will be, the love of my life. I ache for your love every long minute of the day and for every long second of the night. I miss "us" so very much. Was it all just a dream? Was it a dream come true? I can still taste your last long kiss, for your soul was left on my lips. It must have been true love . . . I can still feel your breath on my face as I'm sleeping and the soft touch of your hand on mine as I'm waking, but where are you as I open my eyes? I can feel you next to me as I laugh at something funny and turn to see you laughing also, but you're not there. Where are you? I go calling your name to tell you something I'm thinking, but my voice comes back to me in a cold, shallow echo. Where are you, my love? I am look-ing, searching, calling, crying, crumbling, and crawling to you, but I can't seem to find you anywhere. Where are you? Where did you go? I can't breathe anymore, my love, and I need to feel the rush of your love go through me, touching my spirit once again. I am looking for your eyes in all the faces that go by, but no one ever looks into my soul as your blue eyes looked into mine. Where are you, my love, where are you? I am frantically searching for you and all your love. Each time I came to see you, less and less of "you" would show up at our visits. It was until our last visit that I held on with hope, but you never showed. Some impostor came in your place, thinking he would fool me *into thinking it was you. No matter how much the two of you looked alike, his eyes told me the truth. You were not coming to see me that day, but I sat and talked to the impostor anyway. I've tried to save you, to save us, but I'm losing my grip and slipping down the slope, sliding all the way as I hold on. I must let go to save myself now. Only you can save you, my love. For it is too deep for me, and I fear drowning. It's getting dark and murky, and I can hardly see you way down there. Hello, can you still hear me? Be strong and come back to me, please. Come back up into our love, do whatever it takes, and don't quit the fight for this life. Do it for me and do it for you. I'm begging and pleading, please don't let that place take you away from all of us that love you. You are truly loved by us that know you.*

Paul, I'm so sorry I can't hold on any longer. It's killing me inside to see your sweet love slowly die. I have to say good-bye.

I'll love you always and forever . . .
Cindy

I don't know what to say . . . I thought I might get this "Dear John" letter, but I had no idea that it was going to hurt like this. I'm speechless right now. She was the only good thing left in my life. She was my light at the end of the tunnel. Now what? How do I see where I'm going now? I thought she was my love.

She just punched me in the stomach and left me on the ground, trying to catch my breath. In this most desperate time of need, I've been left behind. But not by these convicts, but by the one that says she loves me. Yes, my heart has become tainted by this place. So what?

It's not like I tried to get tough in here; it just kind of happens to you. Prison has torn many relationships apart, and not just because of the physical separation of the two, but because of the prisoners hardened and broken heart.

The only reason a person hardens their heart is to keep it from falling apart. The flames of anger burn up your sorrow, leaving nothing behind but ash and regret.

Prison is the house of pain. We have good moments here. But they are always filtered through the pain of separation and fear. We are separated from our loved ones, so we feel alone and on our own. We are always on guard and watching for the hungry hunters.

Of course this changes us. Why do you think the recidivism rate is so high? Because we live in the world where PTSD (posttraumatic stress disorder) is the norm. Out there seems a little scary because the world does not live by the "real" rules of life.

Sometimes when I'm thinking about going back out there, it scares me. I'll feel much safer knowing I'm locked up in here, away from the unpredictable world. Crazy I know, but true.

We live on "high alert" all the time, and that's what keeps us safe and alive. We walk calm on the outside, but on the inside, we are "red lining" it. Our RPMs are always maxed out. We're ready for anything at any time. We stay alive living red line on the inside.

My first year inside, I saw the prison therapist. Everyone has to at least once. DOC says so. I kind of liked talking with her, so I saw her twice a week for a few months. She was really nice to talk with and she kind of helped me settle into this new way of life.

She also diagnosed me with having PTSD though at the time, I really didn't know what that meant. Wouldn't anybody coming to prison get it, I asked her. She said, "Most people come to prison already having it, Paul." But she cannot tell you where you might have gotten PTSD. Only that you have it. I really don't seem to notice it. I'm just more alive here at prison than I was out there in the free world. That's all, no big deal.

Anyway, Cindy has left and I don't quite know how to feel, or deal with it. I'm a little pissed the more I think about it, that's for sure. I can't sit in some sorrow pool, bathing in despair. I need to rethink my moves when I get out of here. I could parole out anytime now or do another year. It doesn't really matter. Either way, I'm having a good life when I get out. I'm going for my dreams with or without Cindy.

It's like this . . . Once, there was a man of war. He fought on the battlefield as the good soldier should. He kept his loved ones safe and away from this war and never let the enemy come inside his castle doors. Some days were more bloody then others, but he never give up or gave in. He always returned home to his love; she patched him up like an angel from above. She was his love and life, and he would do anything for her day or night. Then one day, the battle turned around and ran the soldier completely down. He fought fiercely to save his life. Coming home that night, he saw no light. Once inside and locking the door, he called to his love with a loud roar! She was not home. Oh where could she be? Did the enemy come and steal her from me? Then all at once, he felt a sharp pain, and the blood from his body spilled out in vain. The wound was deep and straight into his back. He was puzzled in thought as he lay there bleeding. What sort of enemy was so good at war that they passed right though my heavily locked door? With his last labored breath, he glanced up to see . . . It was betrayal standing there in the dark, crying tears of a broken heart.

Prison can be hard on a man. You really don't think about this kind of stuff going on inside of prison when you're out there. Before I came to prison, I thought it was all about fighting and trying to keep your butt out of trouble. I never thought prison would be harder on my mind and emotions than it would be on my physical well-being, but it is. Prison, the house of wounded hearts.

Well, I think it's time I go get my store for the week. I can't sit here thinking on this anymore today. She's gone.

As I'm walking across the yard, I breathe in and I breathe out. I breathe in, and I breathe out. It seems like it's all still working just fine. I'll keep on moving through this day. Who knows what's left?

As I'm passing through the gate, the guard yells, "Hey, you! Stop." I turn around to see if he's talking to me. "Yeah you, the clean-cut boy!"

"What!" I said. "And don't every call me boy again." I was really pissed.

"Oh, really," he said like a real smart ass. I was standing right in his face at this point, looking him dead in the eyes.

He told me to take a step back from him, and I did. I could get in some serious trouble for that alone. So I took one small step back. "What do you want from me?" he said. "You need to shave before you come this way again."

I could not believe this fish cop. He wanted to give me a hard time out of all the other inmates that needed to shave. Not today, I thought. I had whiskers of a day's time, which is nothing.

"Sure thing, fish," I said. He said nothing in reply. But a smirking look of authority was smeared across his face.

That's why I snapped that day . . . That look on his face. I was about thirty feet away from the gate and almost at the inmate store when I became enraged.

I spun around on my heels to go back to the gate, and this guy Thomas was right there in my face. Where did he come from? He put his hands on my shoulders. "Where are you going so fast, Merk?"

"I'm really pissed, Thomas, and I'm going to beat that cop's ass."

"What?" Thomas said. Thomas is an AB guy, and I really don't know him that well. For him to be talking with me was pretty out of the ordinary. I think we've said hi to each other maybe five times in six months. He knows Johnny and a few other guys I know. This was the longest conversation we've ever had.

"You really don't want to go do that."

"Yes, I do. I want to go hurt him bad. He disrespected me coming through the gate."

Thomas had his hands on my shoulders, keeping my attention on what he had to say. "Listen, Merk, you don't want to do that. Do you know how much time they'll give you if you go kicking his ass?"

"Man, Thomas, I don't care what they do to me."

"Merk, in a hundred years, this won't matter. Do you hear me?"

"I hear you, Thomas."

"Okay, be cool then. I'll see you later." He cracked a smile, leaving me there to contemplate.

I found myself frozen in the moment. I knew my next move would change my life forever . . .

TWENTY SIX

One week . . . and twenty years later.

I just got the bright light in the eyes again. When will they ever stop shining that flashlight in my eyes? Don't they care if someone's trying to sleep? Let me sleep for once, will you. What's that annoying sound?

I just wanted to pull the covers over my head and sleep some more. Then I heard it again. An unfamiliar sound for prison, that's for sure. But where had I heard it before? It was distinctive. I should know its origin, but I can't put my finger on it. I'm still too asleep to know. I really don't care to tell you the truth, just stop it whoever's doing it!

It sounds kind of like . . . Doo da, doo, doo doo, doo. Then again . . . Doo da, doo, doo doo, doo. What? That's all I'm thinking. But it keeps going on and on.

I'm getting pretty upset with this noise. As I'm starting to wake up from a fairly sound sleep, the guard keeps shining his flashlight steady in my face. I can't figure out why he won't stop it.

I put my hand up in front of my face to shield the light as I lift my head off the pillow. That sound is really starting to get to me, and I'm about to grab one of my boots off the floor and throw it at my cell door. This guard has to be a fish. He won't let up on the light or that crazy sound. Wait a minute. What?

I'm now halfway sitting up squinting through my fingers as I try and block as much light as I can. I'm far beyond curious to see

169

who's standing there in the dark and shining that bright light in my face. Then it slowly starts to hit me . . . Wait.

I slowly peek around my hand that's blocking the light. I see two small shadowed figures standing there? What? Two lights in my face? Then quickly, the fog of night lifts, and I remembered all at once.

Like the soft breeze of an open morning window, the sweetest of sounds floats past me. A most perfect and pure whisper, "Daddy, Daddy."

My heart is surrendered.

"Daddy? It's Christmas morning Daddy! Wake up."

"What?" I say.

"Come on, get up, Daddy. It's Christmas Day! Woohoo! Woohoo! It's Christmas morning, Daddy! Time to wake up!"

I'm starting to wake. I can't help but smile. I've just come from the dark side of a long night's sleep. And the bright light of today's world is overwhelming.

Both of my little girls are standing in the doorway of our bedroom, shining their animal flashlights in my eyes and yelling like happy little children do on Christmas morning. I was visiting a bad place last night. But I've already shaken it off, like a wet dog in from the rain.

I still have prison nightmares quite often. I never dream that I'm back there back then. The nightmares are in the present tense. They are pretty much the same theme every time. My family is looking at me through the outer fence of the prison. I can see them well and clear but can never get close to them. It's the scariest nightmare I've ever known.

The noise that I was hearing is from those flashlights we bought them at the zoo. One of them is a hippopotamus, and one is a zebra flashlight. They both open at the mouth when you push on their backs, and the light shines out of their mouths while making the sound of "doo da, doo doo doo doo!"

Madison and Mariah have now jumped onto our bed, bringing the dog with them and are singing the song "Santa Claus Is Coming to Town." Everyone is excited that it's Christmas day. Even the dog is barking. They all roll around on Amanda and myself, wrapped in Christmas bliss.

"Okay, my loves, I'll go down and start the coffee and turn on the Christmas tree lights. Okay everyone?"

"Okay, Dad, but hurry!

As for telling all of you what happened after prison and over the last twenty years. I'm sorry, but it will have to wait for another day. It's Christmas morning, and my little dream girls are waiting for me. Merry Christmas to all and to all a dream life.

I can see through the open double doors of our bedroom the Christmas tree downstairs. The gifts of Christmas love are spilling all around the tree, and the stockings hung over the fireplace are bulging with candy and treats. This day is the birth of our love, so we look within and above as children waiting in awe and belief for a Christmas day so sweet. The snow fell throughout the night and covered the ground with children's delight. Though our home is warmed with all this love, outside it's a cold Alaska morning.

THE END

Facebook: Stonegate A Place Without Time

CPSIA information can be obtained
at www.ICGtesting.com
Printed in the USA
BVOW09s1515180318
510785BV00002B/152/P